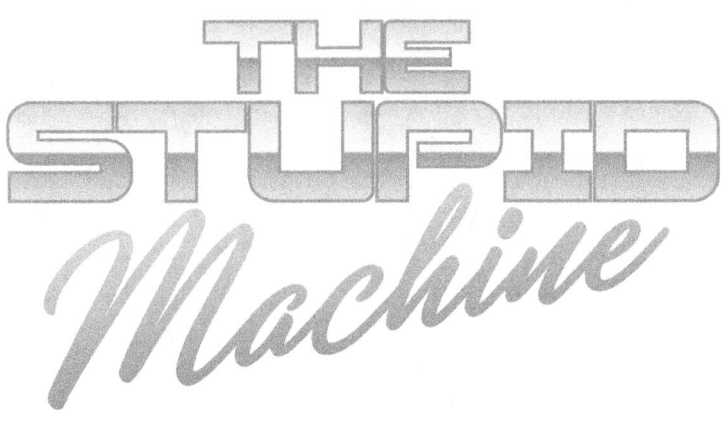

THE STUPID Machine

A.J. schmitz

MAXIXAM
PRESS

For everyone who has supported *this* stupid machine...

...and you know who you are...

...thank you.

Other books by A.J. Schmitz:

Buggin' Out

The Death of Our Dreams: And Other Funny Stories

Nut Job

Dear Norman

Everything in this book is true.

Some of the names have been changed
to protect the stupid.

CONTENTS

GOING DEEP

Ever had a colonoscopy? I highly recommend getting one if you enjoy being starved to the point of delirium and reamed in the ass with a probe. Some people enjoy that kind of invasion. Usually they like to be taken out and given a meal first, but in the end, they enjoy it. Unfortunately, you can't eat before a colonoscopy, so a good meal is out of the question.

My wife had a colonoscopy a full year before I did. She was suffering from abdominal pain and was sent to the gastroenterologist. Dr. Zammer. Nice guy. My father talked about him often because he's gotten a bunch of colonoscopies and knows the ins and outs of the process intimately. Dr. Zammer also goes to our gym, as does my father, and one day he introduced Rita and I to him. Now we see Dr. Zammer all the time, doing lat pulls and bench presses. Anal probing takes strength and the good doctor keeps himself in shape for all the jamming and exploring.

Rita went to Dr. Zammer when these nagging abdominal pains waylaid her gym schedule. Dr. Z pushed and poked her sides and gut, then told her with complete confidence it was a muscle strain, *but*, he would do a colonoscopy and an endoscopy to be absolutely sure. An endoscopy is when they starve you to the point of delirium and send a probe down your throat. So, they poke you from both ends. Kind of like one of those Chinese finger trap toys.

I'm not sure what lucky individual was the first to get a colonoscopy, but it must have been a real adventure.

"Let's clear this person of all their fecal matter and jam a camera up their ass to see what's going on in there."

An endoscopy is less complicated I believe. The throat is a fairly simple tube – a straight shot down to the stomach. Unfortunately, once you reach a certain point, most likely the stomach's exit, you need to go in through the other side.

The ass-end is far more problematic. The intestines are a complicated tube of serpentining caverns. I've heard if you were to lay the intestines out on the ground in a line, they could stretch across multiple states. So sending a camera up there is a delicate matter. It requires a snaking pole – something your average plumber might use to unclog the bathtub. Perhaps more sanitary. But the intestines have more twists and turns than a switchback mountain road. Lots of lefts, rights, ups and downs. I'm not sure how long these probing poles are, but to get it up your rectum might require a team of people feeding it in like a crew of sewer workers stuffing a man into an ancient pipe.

Rita got her colonoscopy first. They striped her naked, probed her, then pushed her into the next room. Some doctors like to do a colonoscopy and endoscopy in the same session. They figure since you're going under anesthesia, do both ends at the same time. Dr. Zammer does his in two separate sessions. He takes an entire day and does asses, then takes a whole different day to do mouths. I suppose it makes sense. You don't want to mix up the equipment. Perhaps there's a chance they send a snake probe down your throat after it's been excavating your colon. Why chance it? Do the procedures on two different days. It's a good philosophy.

After my wife's procedure, the nurse came for me in the waiting room so I could scoop her up and take her home. Rita was snoozing on the gurney like a baby – drooling on herself while her ass poked from her robe. It was actually kind of cute. I shook her awake, but she didn't get up. She kept on snoozing... even snoring... like an old man fishing at a watering hole. After a few more tugs, she awakened and got up to use the bathroom. She planted her feet on the floor and walked right into the wall. Doink! Apparently, it was my job to prevent that type of thing from happening and I failed. After she used the bathroom, she came back and farted like a balloon-testing factory. Then she dressed.

Rita went from seeing Dr. Zammer regularly in the gym, to seeing him regularly in his office because a week later, she had the endoscopy. This procedure wasn't as much fun for me because her ass wasn't hanging out of a robe like the colonoscopy. But, once again, she was snoring like a lumberjack after a long day chopping wood. When Rita goes down, she goes down... like a tranquilized bear.

After all the probing and poking, the doctor was correct – it was a muscle strain. He recommended Rita stop going to the gym for a while and she did. Before she knew it, she was back to normal.

Then it was my turn.

When you have plumbing issues in your home, you call a plumber, who arrives and bends over until their ass-crack is hanging out. When you have plumbing issues with yourself, you call a doctor, go to their office and bend over till your ass crack is hanging out. I didn't have any problems, but I was 50. They say when you reach the age of 50 you need to have a colonoscopy once a year. Who these people are, I don't know, but they deserve a swift kick in the colon. The "they" of the "they say" are most likely the proctologists of the world. They sent this message out into the universe and expanded their business model 1,000% and probably more. I was past 51 and had pushed my recommended colonoscopy off for far too long. One day while doing the leg press machine at the gym, Dr. Zammer told me it was time to get the colonoscopy. He said it with such conviction, I almost felt shame. But, then he followed it with a warm smile, so I felt comforted knowing he'd be the one to do the dirty deed. Then he went to the bicep machine and did curls.

After a quiet consultation with Dr. Zammer that entailed questions about my diet and alcohol intake (all of which was too much and too heavy) he punched me in for a colonoscopy. The appointment was in two months. Apparently there was a logjam of people needing the procedure.

I'm not sure how one gets into the practice of gastroenterology or proctology. I know when doctors are in medical school, at some point they have to get into a specialty…

focus on a particular part of the body and master it. I assume they discuss it with their fellow students. "I'm going to be a Cardiologist" (heart doctor) they might say out loud. Or a Neurologist (nervous system); an Endocrinologist (hormones and glands); or a Pediatrician (children's doctor) and so on.

How does one discover they want to focus on the gastrointestinal system knowing they'll be dealing with a bunch of assholes? Literally. Are they into asses? Or ass play? Anal sex? Do other interns at the hospital make fun of them? Obviously it's a much-needed profession. All of them are.

There's also the other end of the spectrum. The blustery, stinky entrance hole. The mouth. There's vomit, rotten teeth and halitosis. Thank God for the surgical mask – blocker of germs and foul odors. I know dentists stare into some dark caverns full of rotten teeth, but what if those mouths are vomiting, burping and retching? After a few years of people's rancid insides coming out in the form of liquid, you might question your career choices. Your mind wanders back to the crossroads of life where you decided to go from Podiatrist (foot doctor), to Proctologist (ass doctor). Feet can be smelly slabs of flesh. Trust me, I've been to the beach where people's cloven hooves are on full display when in actuality they should be lopped off at the calf. But there *has* to come a time when your chosen field of gastroenterology is questioned... even a little bit. Opening a skull and tinkering around the brain is pretty stressful, and dealing with people who are dying of cancer could be depressing, but daily doses of bile and gas could drive one over the edge of sanity.

The passion for their work could be personal as well. Their parent was a proctologist, or their relative died from stomach issues, which drove them to help those with similar issues. My father was an architect, which made me want to be a writer. Go figure. It's a profession I question almost on the hour.

To prepare for my Thursday colonoscopy, I stopped eating at 9:00pm Tuesday evening and fasted. Last thing I jammed in my face was an ice cream cone. I remember it fondly because I went 40 hours without a morsel of food until my colonoscopy. Honestly, the fast wasn't that bad. The worst part is the terrible elixir they make you drink to clean out your digestive system. It tastes like powered lemonade mixed with seawater. The kind of seawater with bits of seaweed and crab shells floating inside of it. Sea-salt is an appetizing additive to things like caramel and chocolate, not lemonade.

When Rita did her fast and cleanse, she puked half the colon cleanser while drinking it. I managed to get it down without vomiting, but it wasn't easy. Certainly not pleasant… unless you enjoy seawater. Most people spit seawater out when they get the slightest bit in their mouth wading in the ocean. Those of us getting a colonoscopy are forced to chug it by the carafe. Not only that, it's unnaturally chemically. I've swallowed pool water with less chemicals than this colon cleanse. So, not only is it powdered lemonade mixed with seawater, but it's sweetened with pool chemicals. By the time you're done choking the potion down your empty stomach, you feel like a hollow cavity. You'll know immediately how the kitchen sink feels after you dump a gallon of Liquid Drano to move a clump of hair through its twisty pipes.

Then, the real fun starts. The evil elixir you chugged

converts all the solid waste in your body into liquid, which explodes out of your asshole at the rate of about 1 liter per minute. They suggest you drink lots of water during the process and you know exactly why. It comes out in such large quantities you begin to wonder how much liquid your intestinal track can hold. The human body can do so many wondrous and ridiculous things, but chemistry can make it perform many things it doesn't normally do. Like full liquid waste evacuation till you're peeing out of your anus. To complete the dreadful process, after a restless night of sleep on an empty stomach, I awaked before the sun to chug another container of sea salt lemonade. It's not a great replacement for coffee.

By the time my 10:30 appointment rolled around, my mood had flipped from diligence to displeasure. After my wife's 18th ass joke, I'd had enough. I wanted to be probed and home in my normal routine, drinking coffee and eating something ridiculously greasy and potentially heart-stopping. Take away my food and I'll get by. Take away my coffee and someone could lose a limb. Maybe even me.

I arrived to my appointment on time, as I often do, and was met with a gust of wind and the smell of sage or maybe even marijuana, which I found unusual. Normally the office has the faint smell of diarrhea, which is to be expected with this type of work. A mechanic's garage smells like oil, and a gastroenterologist's office smells like a butt crack. The smell of something burning was a pleasant change.

When I checked in, my wife told me that the pretty brunette woman sitting and smiling in the corner of the waiting room was Dr. Zammer's wife, so perhaps she came in that day and put her stamp on the place – popped open some air fresheners, cranked on some fans and sparked up some Purple Haze. I don't know. I don't judge. I would have partaken in a puff or two myself, but that would have made me hungrier than I already was. Maybe Dr. Zammer was puffing on some sticky Kush, which makes his work more tolerable. Usually I like my doctors sober when they're doing work on me, especially anal probes, but hey, whatever gets you through the day.

After I undressed and got my ass hanging out of the provided robe, I laid on a gurney and spoke with the anesthesiologist. Dr. Waller. Super nice. He asked me a few questions like: "you're here for a colonoscopy?" and I assured him I was. I'm glad we had that conversation because it's possible I could have awoken to find they'd amputated my left leg. I've seen things like that on the news before. Guy goes in for surgery on his right leg, comes out with his left leg missing. I didn't go in for surgery, but like I said before, we don't want something going in the mouth that was previously in someone's ass. Especially if the doctors have been blazing blunts in the other room.

After some light banter, I told the doctor about my debilitating Trypanophobia and Vasovagal. That's the fear of needles in a medical setting. I don't mind shots or even needles themselves, it's when they go into my vein. When having blood drawn, I turn into a puddle of tears. I've even broken down at the blood bank like a person in the throes of a bad hallucinogenic trip. Usually my wife is there to hold my hand, but this time she couldn't as I was in a secure area where asses and potentially genitalia were out in the open air. But, the anesthesiologist's hands were like butter and he punctured the vein without any mental or physical breakdown from me.

Dr. Zammer entered with a big smile and asked me why I wasn't at the gym and I told him I had a doctor's appointment. We laughed, and the next thing I knew, I was waking up alone in the recovery room with terrible abdominal pains. After my wife came in, I asked her to get the nurse who called the doctor to check on me.

Dr. Z assured me that he didn't puncture the walls of my intestines or leave a pair of forceps in my colon or anything like that. It was just gas. But he did say that the nurse had trouble navigating my intestines.

"You have very curvy intestines with difficult angles." He said.

I assumed everyone's intestines were pretty much the same – like the intestines you see on human body charts with pink tubes bending around the body. Apparently mine are unique in the bad way. Not only that, I didn't realize a nurse was in the room with me.

"She really had to use a lot of force to get the camera inside." He said.

I pictured her with one foot on my head, knocking the probe into my ass with a croquet mallet. Usually you don't want to hear the term 'force' in regards to something going deep inside your anus. I'm not a porn star, but I assume there's a point where the pleasure turns to pain. Maybe around the three-foot mark? I don't know.

After a trip to the bathroom, Dr. Zammer had me back on the gurney, flipping me from side to side like a marinated pork loin. It felt as if a loaf of bread was rising in my gut. I then released a fart that lasted, without the least bit of exaggeration, about 8 seconds. Rita said "wow" and the doctor assured me he heard that all the time.

"That's music to my ears." He said jovially.

Apparently Dr. Zammer has never had the pleasure of listening to The Beatles, James Brown or even Rebecca Black, all of them creating sounds more appealing than two ass cheeks slapping together in successive pulses.

Before he exited, the doctor told me they had to remove a fairly large polyp that: "could have been potentially cancerous" which means I'll be forced to do this routine every year till I die. At the checkout, the nurse told me to drink water and take it easy.

"Eat light and don't drink any alcohol. You can return to normal activities tomorrow."

I figured her recovery plan was merely a "suggestion." I went home and had two waffles with peanut butter, two coffees, a cheese omelette with rice, a bag of tortilla chips, some more cheese, three slices of pizza, a salad, cherry pie with vanilla ice cream, and washed it down with a couple glasses of red wine.

THE STUPID MACHINE

If there was truly an intelligent, remorseful and caring God, why did he create the clumsy, irrational and stupid machine known as the human being? Basically a thinking pig, the human runs on electricity and sugar. It's smart enough to create complex philosophy, but dumb enough to debate its merits on Facebook.

It takes the average human about 20 years to figure out what the hell it's doing, then starts its fast decent into obsolesce by being a lazy, confused and perpetually stumbling bag of bones, addicted to everything that passes over its lips. It wants to procreate faster than it dies, burn everything to the ground in its path, and leave nothing but a remorseful wake of destruction behind it. And those are the good attributes!

Have you ever thought about the amount of food humans eat just to get through one simple day? If we're lucky we sleep eight solid hours. That leaves us 16 waking hours to screw things up. Those 16 hours are spent either working or preparing food to shovel into our loud, fat faces. We can barely go two hours without the need to feed our screaming, rumbling bellies.

After we wake up in the morning, we eat breakfast. Going eight minuscule hours is considered a FAST in our pitiful existence. Go a full day without eating and most people would consider that torture. Anyway, we wake up and eat breakFAST... guzzle coffee or tea, toast, eggs, ham, and half a goddamn farm. Then, after we've done the Herculean task of washing ourselves and dressing, we basically need another meal. We can't go more than two hours without a wheelbarrow full of food to stuff into our faces or we pass out on the ground, virtually unable to complete the simplest task. We can't file papers, create art or use any machinery until we're fed.

Sometimes we substitute food with caffeine. Coffee, tea, Red Bull... whatever electrical stimulant we need to get us to our next meal. We chug these liquids that drive us for 30 minutes, then, when the false stimulants wear off, we're twice as empty and we're STARVING. It's time for lunch. Breakfast was literally about five minutes ago, but screw it, we need a full sit-down meal with cutlery and steaming meats and vegetables.

In many countries, lunch is the biggest meal of the day. They eat massive portions until they pass out for two or three hours. Then they awaken, resume business for 15 minutes, shutter everything, and prepare for dinner. Some of the women in these countries are very traditional. They chop, slice and cook food all day to feed their families. Some of them have never seen a room besides the kitchen. They step outside into the yard and believe they've gone to heaven. It's that bad. The only water view they've ever seen is a boiling pot.

In the United States, we eat while we work, which has made the Gastrointestinal industry billion and billions of dollars. While jamming a burrito into the screaming hole known as our mouth with one hand, we type with the other hand, while our bosses shout in both ears. The only hole in our body that is not being assaulted is the asshole, but even that orifice knows it will be assaulted later when it shoots the half-digested burrito out of its sore exit. The urethra is being assaulted because it's holding back a dam full of coffee that went through the body like water through an arid houseplant.

The satiation of lunch lasts about an hour. By three in the afternoon, we're thinking about food again. So, we have a snack. Cookies, coffee… more sugar. We need high-levels of fat so our furnaces can process this gunk and turn it into a raging fuel that propels us like jet engines to the five O'clock whistle. The millisecond work stops, we think "what's for dinner?" For the love of all that is holy, we can't go more than FIVE minutes without planning, debating or thinking about what we're eating, or where our next meal is coming from. It's sad. If you go to the bar after work and drink alcohol, that can curb your monstrous appetite for a bit, but then you'll need to feed the beast. Take out food is always nice. But what everyone needs is a good, old-fashioned, home-cooked meal. We're baking and frying and sautéing and running around the kitchen with deadly sharp knives and glowing red metal and fire and preparing our food. We've got to eat. We're starving!!!!!!

Eventually it's ready and we sit and funnel the food into our heads like vacuum cleaners. We laugh because "it takes hours to cook and minutes to eat" as we slump into temporary comas. Then, we must clean the mess we made. There's flour on the floor and gravy on the wall. In our spastic passion to feed our bottomless pits, we massacred our kitchens. It takes hours to clean and we hit the couch exhausted. By the time we click on the TV, we're ravenous. Washing the pots and scrubbing the table has left a hole in our gullets the size of the Grand Canyon. We need to eat! So we have dessert. Ice cream, cookies and cake. Just a little something for the "sweet tooth" – a little treat to help us fall asleep – piles of refined sugar and chocolate. The PERFECT sleeping aid.

Before electricity, everyone ate meals with the sunlight. Dinner was eaten at three or four in the afternoon and then everyone retired to the dining room as the sun went down for "supper." That was a fourth... or fifth meal of the day. I've lost track at this point. They said: "we're going to bed in an hour? Let's eat a meal. We don't want to wake up in the middle of the night STARVING! Let's eat now." So they ate. Whatever was leftover after eating dinner. Cold chicken, potatoes, half a hog on heavy breads. Just something light to tide them over until morning. Then they'd eat warm puddings, coagulated cream cakes, and lard on crackers. Most people didn't live past 40 years-old before the civil war. It's amazing the human race is still standing.

As the digestion process takes over, the fats coat the heart in slabs of deadly plaque while the sugars flood the brain like lightning. The internal combustion engine cranks into overdrive – expelling gas from every free orifice in horn-blasting intensity as every valve, gland and node secretes enzymes to break it all into bricks. The insatiable appetite is not the only flaw of the Stupid Machine. Because we impact our internal tubes with stacks of food and pitchers of liquid on a daily basis just to walk a few steps, we constantly need to discard all this shit.

The Stupid Machine has to expel waste all day and night. Health experts say: "drink plenty of water" which means you'll be in the bathroom all day. When we're not stuffing food in our faces in the kitchen, we're in the bathroom punching it out. It's amazing we accomplish anything at all. People need to urinate about 20 times a day. You can't go anywhere without the panic of knowing where to piss. Walk through a city or get in a car and the first thing you think about is where you're going to dispose of all this waste. You'll get a ticket if you drop your pants and go in the street, so you need a bathroom. A department store, gas station... a restaurant where "Customers Only" are allowed to use the facilities. Anywhere. Public bathrooms are few and far between. In many cases a homeless person has made a small chalet out of them. You enter and you smell the distinct odor of someone who hasn't bathed in a year. It's hard to drop freight and loosen the hose when your shitting in someone's living room. Bathrooms are precious on the road.

The intake and outtakes systems are not the Stupid Machine's only issues. We seem to be dying of every disease ever created, whether by God or from our own incompetent hand. As science becomes more prolific, we're identifying diseases at the rate of about ten per hour. Humans are getting cut down like gazelle on the plains. Cancer seems to be an enjoyable diagnosis at this point. People love to exclaim how the Stupid Machine is a marvel of engineering. "Isn't the human body incredible?" they chime. It has about 5,000 different organs in it, each one ready to shut down or break in some complicated, expensive way. The dog is essentially a mouth, stomach and asshole. It can eat a pile of tin cans and not blink an eye. The Stupid Machine eats one un-ripened blueberry and it needs to hit the urgent care center in a speeding ambulance.

There's so many people on the news whose illnesses still need to be identified, the only way to track them is through Go Fund Me pages. Doctors need to add three more years to their doctorate degrees to keep up with this madness. Many of the issues are brought on by our terrible diets and from the chemicals we spray on everything we touch. Bathroom cleaners, furniture polish, counter top disinfectants, weed killer and insecticides. God forbid we should eat a bug! We may get a dose of pure protein. Serve up another helping of aorta jamming cheese on coagulated meat patties with sugar buns!

The Stupid Machine needs to get these internal issues under control. Our veins are congested, our organs are underperforming, our sinuses are draining uncontrollably and our intestines are calamitous chutes filled with unimaginable discharges that are either going too much, or not enough. There's so many medicines that Big Phar TV commercials dominate the airwaves. The medicines consist of names that live at the end of the alphabet. They have multiple Xs and Zs and the logo has swooshes and dots over them. These pills stop shaking and quaking, help you go or stop you from going. The side effects are worse than the problem. If you're gobbling handfuls of pills where the main side effect is death, you may need to rethink your choices.

A simple check-up is a cause for alarm. The fat in your heart is too high and the sugar levels are too low. We get to a certain age and they need to probe you from every direction. Tubes go down your throat and cameras go up your ass. Of course, the Stupid Machine is so complicated, it's under constant need of medication to get it up and running correctly. The brain juices are misfiring, the pancreas isn't secreting and the major organs are rattling inside the cavity like toddlers drumming on pots and pans. To remedy these self-inflicted issues, we're given handfuls of pills that potentially reverse the problems, but may or may not have the side effects of:

Diarrhea

Constipation

Nausea

Vomiting

Abdominal pain

Cough

Shortness of breath

Upper respiratory tract infection

Weakness

Headache

Gas

Heartburn

Nightmares

Sleep disturbances

Sleepwalking

Insomnia

Black, tarry stools

Bloody nose

Bloody or cloudy urine

Pain in muscles, bones, and joints

Rash

Itchy skin

Skin irritation

Skin blistering or peeling

Swelling

Decreased appetite

Back pain

Neck pain

Fever

Urinary tract infection

New or worsening cough

Chest pain

Cardiovascular events

Chest pain, pressure, or squeezing

Difficulty speaking

Dizziness

Drowsiness

Hoarseness

Loss of consciousness

Seizures

Trouble swallowing

Aggression or agitation

Anxiety

Delusions

Depression

Hostility

Mania

Hallucinations

Panic

Suicidal thoughts

Psychosis

Paranoia

Homicidal ideation

Suicidal ideation

Ringing or buzzing in the ears

Fruit-like breath odor

Groin or scrotum pain

Inability to have or keep an erection

Painful, permanent erection

Unusual urges for sex and gambling

Loss of smell

Increased body movements

Increased sensitivity to light

Increased sensitivity to touch or pain

Increased thirst

Increased urination

Loss of bladder control

Loss of sexual ability, drive, or desire

Menstrual bleeding occurring earlier or lasting longer than usual

Mental depression

Nervousness

Memory Loss

Wanting to crawl out of your skin

Pale skin

Nails falling off

Slurred speech

Swollen lymph glands

Unable to move face

Unusual bleeding or bruising

Frequent bowel movements

Severe abdominal pain or tenderness

Yellowing of your skin

Yellowing of the eyes

Eye sensitivity to light

Eye problems

Rapid heartbeat

Increased sweating

Loss of appetite

Weight gain

Weight loss

Feeling more hungry or thirsty than usual

Urinating more often than usual

Hair loss

Feeling cold

Chills or shaking

Your voice gets deeper

Fainting

Forgetfulness

Decrease in your amount of urine

Blood Clots

Compulsive Behaviors

Birth Defects

Swelling of your ankles

Blurry vision

Eye pain or redness

Flushing

Wheezing

Feel like passing out

Fever

Cancer

...and the aforementioned *Death*

And this is just the tip of the iceberg. There's so many side effects it makes Leo Tolstoy's *War and Peace* read like a postcard. They can't possibly fit them all on a bottle, so they continue them on their website where you scroll for eternity until you reach the end of the internet.

The Stupid Machine is able to scale the highest mountain, fly to space, and run, swim and bike a hundred miles in Iron Man competitions, yet we're incapable of fighting the common cold. This tiny germ hits us and we're down for the count. Two days in bed and enough liquids to flood the Sahara. We eat soup and sleep till it passes. The Flu is even worse. This bug enters our system and we're crippled for a week, if not more. We puke into buckets and our house is quarantined. Covid-19 is a walk in the park compared to what's coming over the horizon. We've eradicated the black plague but others are probably ready to pounce. What color is scarier than black? Orange... green... red? The red plague? It's the stuff of science fiction but it's based in reality.

The only thing we haven't done is eaten each other in droves of cannibalism. It's unsanitary because of the diseases we carry, but mainly because it's considered impolite. The Stupid Machine is sacred and to be eaten by another Stupid Machine is frowned upon. Other animals are considered sacred as well. Horses, dogs, cats and I suppose bald eagles as well. We have more than enough to eat, but watch your back any way. Everything else is fair game. Cows, chickens, fish... all the other animal machines that roam the earth. We stew 'em, grind 'em... mash them into paste. We form them into nuggets and inhale them as a snack.

Diseases tend to jump from animals to humans. We have chicken pox and monkey pox and other kinds of pox. Small pox are coming back because people don't want to be vaccinated. These idiots prefer to take their chances and those are slim odds. We like to use animals as test subjects, which is cruel and unusual, but; who else are we going to test them on? People? Humans are sacred apparently and can't be experimented on. We'll drop miles of acid, smoke a house-fire of cigarettes, and chug oceans of alcohol but stick a needle in people for the good of medical science and you might as well tell them they're being injected with pure, unfiltered Satan.

The Stupid Machine is just an animal and people forget that. We look, smell and act like animals all the time. Most of us have too much hair or not enough. The people that have too much have it growing on their backs or ass. The one's that have too little are deficient on their top of their heads. Women especially. They shower and yank clumps of hair out and panic. The blobs of wet fur resemble a small rodent and they scream in terror. As you get older, hair comes from everywhere you don't want it... out of the ears, out of the nostrils, and on places you didn't think hair could grow. My eyebrows grow mutant hairs that need hedge-clippers to chop. I used to have hair under my armpits, but now the hair has disappearing and is growing out of my shoulder. Like weeds. Hairs spring out of the nipples, the top of the ears, the side of the neck and the tip of the nose. If you don't maintain it, you could wake one night and be mistaken for a werewolf. Of course we need to wash the filthy beast. We can't go more than a few hours without washing because the food and drink we jammed down our gullets is pouring out of the holes of our skin.

The Stupid Machine basically has about five good years in it before it falls apart. By the time you figure life out, you're essentially worthless as a functioning being. Your bones are cracking, there's hair everywhere and the skin hangs like cheap window drapes. They say "youth is wasted on the young" and that's dead-on accurate. You say to yourself: "I get it now! I figured it out! I can conquer the world!" but you're essentially in a chair, unable to move because you're breaking down like a jack-o-lantern in December. When you're young, life is moving along just fine, then you hit the summit and it's a speeding crash towards your inevitable death. If you're lucky, you'll go out in a fiery blaze, but you're more likely to collapse in a never-ending series of breakdowns till they put you out of your misery in the hospital. Unfortunately, the Stupid Machine doesn't want to go out like that. The Stupid Machine is basically dying its whole life but by the time it's time to drop in the coffin, it wants to hang on for dear life. It fights the good fight, clinging to the last bit of precious existence.

I recently went to a funeral and it was a morbid experience. I told my wife that when I die, I want a beach party. When she asked: "What if you die in the winter?" I said, "ski party."

They'll take my cremated ashes and scatter them on the ground. I want a Ska band to play like maniacs and everyone in attendance will be required to dance until they're exhausted and my ashes have been pounded into the earth like a cheap cigarette. We'll serve beer and wine and tequila, and everyone will party till they puke. A good party is just about the only thing the Stupid Machine is good for.

EIGHT EYES TO SEE YOU

For my entire life, I had eagle-eye vision. 20/20 vision. 10/20 vision. X-ray vision. Okay, I didn't have X-ray vision, but as the band *The Who* once said... I could see for miles and miles. On road trips, my father would state the name of the road we needed to find, and I'd squeeze my head between the front seats and read the street sign so far in advance my father would become incensed.

"You can read that?" He'd shout in disbelief.

"Yeah." I'd say confused, as if everyone could see a two-foot wide street sign 150 yards away that was also partially obscured by a tree branch.

Growing up, everyone in my house wore glasses except me. My mother was born wearing glasses and her eyesight deteriorated as the years went on. My father and sister wore reading glasses as long as I can remember. They went to opticians and held books inches from their faces in astonishingly bright light. I would hold a book on my lap and read without any magnified eyewear in a room so dark, you could develop photographs. My mother would enter, flip on the light and ask: "How can you see anything?" I'd shrug and continue reading, the page not any clearer than it was before the light came on. At the doctor, I'd be asked to read the fifth line on the eye chart and I'd recite the name of the eye chart company as well as the address and phone number where you could order more eye charts. My eyesight was *that* good.

As I got older, I realized that not everyone had this incredible ability. My friends wore glasses and were constantly cleaning them or carefully sticking contact lenses to their exposed eyeballs. I never thought much about it. I lived a carefree life where the only thing I needed to grab before I walked out the door were the keys to my car. Eventually the cluster of things I needed to grab on the way into the daily grind grew. Car keys and a wallet, but also cigarettes, a lighter and other random things I was culturally tied to… building passes, subway cards and other tokens of entry.

Having quit smoking, I was free of just about everything other than keys and a wallet again – and even those were streamlined. My wallet lightened its load as the times changed. The quarter I kept for the emergency phone call disappeared, but the cell phone was added to the mix. But the cell held credit card numbers and other modern conveniences, so the wallet lightened once again. And there I was, living a completely carefree life, roaming the world and seeing everything clearly, like a hawk searching for its inevitable prey.

And then it all came to a crashing halt.

Like a two-ton steel door, my beautiful ability to see clearly slammed shut. In the course of about two weeks, my eyesight went from eagle to feeble. It was devastating. Street signs I could mark from a football field away, wouldn't come into focus until I was literally under them, and by then, some asshole was behind me, leaning on his horn, curious as to why I'd stopped my car in the middle of the road. Books that I read in the dark couldn't be seen unless I held a spotlight to them, and my cell phone was basically a glowing rectangle in my hand. It was brutal.

I was told this is a common occurrence to the elderly. The old. Those who are quickly turning to dust. It's a subset of humans known as the 40 and above crowd. At the ripe old age of 44, my eyes went from sparkling, crystal balls of foresight, into dull, opaque balls of blindness. I was squinting at the dinner table, squinting in the sun, and squinting when a blurry human figure was approaching me calling my name. The only thing that came in sharp relief was the fact I needed glasses.

I went to the optician and he confirmed that my eyesight sucked. He didn't use those exact words, but I knew that's what he was thinking. Asking me to read the fifth line on the eye chart, he found that I'd confused all my Cs with O's, My Fs with E's and Vs with Ws. A test I passed with flying colors as a kid, I now failed with paultry greys as an adult. It was a sad day indeed. I stuck my face in a series of machines to confirm the suckiness. I looked at a hot air balloon and it told me I didn't have ocular cancer, which was a huge plus. My doctor also used that giant black eyesight tester with the little glass flippy lenses – the ungainly titled Phoroptor – which sounds like a dinosaur with a camera. It's only benefit, besides testing your eyesight, is that you temporarily look like Catwoman at a New Year's Eve masked ball. My doctor asked what was better "4 or 5?" ... 7 or 8?" until the right combination of clarity became clear.

Afterwards, the doctor sold me some ugly square frames that cost more than a pair of black market retinas. They were *that* expensive. I believe I'm still paying them off. Apparently the eyewear frame industry is a scam. They take 2 bucks worth of plastic, twist them into loops and charge $300 for them. It's a monopoly... run by small, balding men like the Monopoly Man in the board game *Monopoly*, except he wore a monocle, which is one of the least effective forms of eyewear I can think of. Unless he had bad eyesight in only one eye, then it sort of makes sense. But you have to jam a monocle into the crevice of your orbital bone, which is incredibly uncomfortable, so you might as well use bifocals, even if you only need the one focal. Of course, a monocle is probably cheaper... maybe half the price... so there's savings involved. But the Monopoly Man is carrying a giant sack of cash on his back, so money doesn't seem to be the issue with him. It's definitely an issue with me. Bad eyesight is costly.

Unfortunately, I had a full-eye malfunction, requiring not only glasses for distance (Near-sighted) but for seeing up-close as well (Far-sighted). How these two terms became the norm, I'm not sure, but when someone tells me they're near-sighted, it takes me about three minutes to figure out what it all means. Like a double negative... or even a triple negative. It's definitely nothing I don't not understand. As it stands, I'm nothing-sighted. I cannot see you far away, I cannot see you two feet away. I cannot see you here or there, I cannot see you anywhere. Because of this terrible malady I need not one, but *two* pairs of glasses.

My days of simply jamming a set of keys, a wallet, and a phone into my pockets are long gone. I now double-fist two eyeglass cases, or I do the next best thing and jam a pair of glasses into my shirt collar, freeing one hand to do a task like driving or using a hose. Of course I bend over and the pair of glasses in my shirt collar falls to the hard ground, lenses down, until they're scratched beyond simply buffing them out. I contemplated an eyeglass chain, but I refuse to go so far as to delve into the territory of an 80 year-old man. That's where I draw the line. I have some self-respect.

Unfortunately, the madness didn't stop there. My close range glasses were perfect for the computer, but they didn't cut it for reading, so I was forced to buy reading glasses. So yes, I now own *three* pairs of glasses. It's absurd. I have them jammed in my shirt collar, in my pockets, and on top of my head. I swap them out like a magician doing card tricks for whatever occasion is appropriate. Sometimes I'll get caught in the middle of a situation where I'm unsure what pair I need. Is that sign 8 feet away or 3 feet away? Which pair do I go with? I've swapped them back and forth, unable to determine which is right. Sometimes I'll be wearing my readers and wonder why I can't see the car that pulled into my driveway, then the next minute I'll look at my computer and it's a jagged set of shapes that induces a migraine headache.

Once in a while I'll find myself with all three pairs of glasses on my face, which crosses over into a Picasso painting. I'll watch one unknown New York Knickerbocker toss a basketball into a hoop through one pair, then look down and read something with another pair teetering on the tip of my nose, while talking to my son with the middle pair in the middle of my nose. These three pairs inevitable cross streams and I'll have a pair OVER another pair, creating a new and exciting prescription. I look around to see what objects are in focus, and what objects have turned into cloudy blurs.

Because I didn't need glasses until I was 44, I went a really long time without them being part of my DNA. No matter how hard I try, I can't seem to remember to bring them with me. I'm speeding down the road in the car and realize I can't see a freakin' thing. I could potentially kill someone. Then I have to squint the whole time, which causes another migraine. Many times people will stick their phone in my face to show me a hilarious video and I can't find my glasses. "Where did I put them?" I say, cursing myself. I usually put them down somewhere dumb, like the stove... or they're on top of my head for the 50th time that week. It' a never-ending struggle to incorporate them into my life. I leave them at home, I leave them in the car, I leave them at people's houses, and I leave them in bars.

Sighted-people are also intolerant of people who can't see. They show you cute pictures of their dog and when you tell them you can't see, they become angry. They push their cell phone closer, but all that does is make the screen brighter. These types of eye issues have been known to ruin friendships.

I've contemplated Lasik surgery, but it's too expensive and I'd be the 1 in 50,000 that gets permanent eye damage. I love Stevie Wonder, but I don't want to emulate his look. Sunglasses and beaded dreadlocks are not my thing. My job requires that I use my eyes... most people's jobs do... but not being able to create art would be devastating. Writing books may work out. I could dictate to an assistant about my twisted life, sorted affairs and terrible philosophies, but my wife would quickly tire of listening to me.

Looking for my lost glasses has become a sport unto itself. 25% of the time I'm wearing them over my actual eyes. The other 25% they're on top of my head. But the other 50% is a crapshoot. Like looking for the car keys, they could be just about anywhere… the bathroom, in the refrigerator, and most likely on a table the same color as the frames so as to become completely camouflaged, only to be seen when the lenses catch the light at an angle. The only way to truly find them is to draft someone with good eyesight to hunt with you. Like my son. He looks, but he can't find anything, even if he's standing on it, so he's of no use. People give the advice: "re-trace your steps" but that is usually worthless advice because my life is a series of chaotic moments and when I do find the glasses on the stairs or inside a grocery bag, I realize I was blacking out due to rage or confusion and dumped them like a drug bust.

Like most things, glasses need to be cleaned. Con-stantly. When they're not covered in bacon grease from my greasy fingers, they're covered in grease from my greasy face. They have fingerprints, smudges, smears and particles of things like toothpaste, yogurt, mud, and anything you tried to open that contains liquid. If you clean your glasses till they're spotless, you're guaranteed to drop them (lenses down of course) and pick them up with your fat, greasy thumb in the middle of the lens. It doesn't matter how careful you are, you still pick them up with the lens. Mostly because you can't see. If someone picks them up for you, they'll do it with their greasy hand and return them to you with their finger AND palm prints. You can use these imprints to have them arrested or steal their identity.

Someday I'll be simpatico with my glasses. I won't forget them at home. I won't put them in a random spot and I might bite the bullet and get a chain to keep them from sliding off my shirt and hitting the pavement.

Perhaps, if I ever scrape enough money together, I'll get the laser surgery. Then my eyes can be razor sharp and in-focus. Or, I can wait and get a full eyeball transplant that is equipped with built in monitors for watching television.

TRAFFIC CIRCLE

My town tore out an old 5-way intersection that was a certifiable deathtrap and replaced it with a sensible, easy-going traffic circle. The residents then had a certifiable conniption fit – driven absolutely bonkers by the change. It was a mass of confusion and piles of crumpled, smoking cars. People drove in clockwise while others drove counter clockwise, all while people plowed through the circle like it didn't even exist. People came at it from every conceivable direction except the direction it was intended for.

In Europe, they've been using traffic circles (AKA Roundabouts) since Julius Caesar was in diapers, but they built one in my town and everyone's brain seized like the engine of a 1958 Edsel. Suddenly, everyone forgot their DMV handbooks and flew through the circular thing-a-ma-bob like a flying circus – with the greatest of unease – bounding over embankments, into the air, like Evel Knievel and his fabulous flying machines… jumping through fiery hoops of wonder like a monster truck show.

Because the town folk were so terribly confused, they needed to put signs all around the god-forsaken circle. So many gleaming signs it's laughable. There is, without one hint of exaggeration, about 50 signs posted around this stupid traffic circle. Since five roads enter it, it's necessary to tell the motorist where the hell they're going at all five entry points. There's a sign for each road and whether the motorist is going north and south on it. That's ten signs right there. Then there's a speed limit sign for the idiots who're hitting the traffic circle like they're driving off a cliff without brakes. That's another five. Then, for some unknown reason, there's merge signs, yield signs, yardage markers and since there's a hospital within spitting distance, there's a few blue signs that simply say H.

But, there's more! Since many of the morons screaming through town need to be told that a traffic circle is immanent, they have yellow reflectors encircling it like candles on a birthday cake. Your headlights flash across the circle and it lights up like a freakin' Christmas tree. Like a firework show. Many people think they've accidentally driven onto an airport landing strip. If a tarmac guy with those flashlight cones waved you through, you wouldn't bat an eye.

To make matters worse, there's another identical traffic circle about 100 feet away and it has all the bells and whistles like the one I just described. This circle also has 5 intersections pooling into it. I believe the human circulatory system is less complicated than this geometric conglomeration, and the human heart has less valves, pipes and chambers than this ridiculous system of converging routes. Yet, somehow, it all makes sense. It's much safer than the previous nightmare of converging roads, but still, car tires can be heard screeching through the traffic circle from miles around. You'd think it was the Indy 500, but it's just people going for milk. People hit the traffic circles so fast, you can feel the G force from your car. The Apollo 11 astronauts had less stress-testing than the average child in the backseat of their parent's vehicle.

Entering the traffic circle is now the ultimate game of chicken. People plow into the circle like an avalanche of boulders down the Matterhorn. They rumble in as though life has lost all meaning and if death is the answer to the traffic circle's question, then so be it. No one slows or yields in any way, shape, or form even though there's 20 yield signs. They just zip in, life and auto insurance be damned. Their SUVs are strong enough to handle a bazooka to the side, so a fender bender or a complete rollover is nothing but a minor inconvenience.

Before the traffic circle existed, the area was a bizarre knot of traffic lights and weird stop signs. The circles are super smooth, but the patience to wait has been eliminated with the traffic lights. People blast into the circle even though it's full of spinning cars… twirling around like a washing machine spin cycle. They jam themselves in at top speed at the very hint of open space… like ball-bearings falling into the open chambers of a never-ending Rube Goldberg machine. God forbid they wait a fraction of a second and make a safe and responsible traffic movement. Before, people had to wait in traffic lights, but now, to tap the break for one second before entering the circle would be considered a failure of forward momentum. The only time someone stops is if their life is flashing before their eyes. They know that to enter the circle means certain death, so they slam the brakes and curse the person in the traffic circle for making them grind to a halt.

As soon as they built this marvel of engineering, they had to pretty much tear the thing up and start over. Back when it was an eye-sore of traffic-grinding stoplights and sadness, the area would flood like a Pan-Asian country during monsoon season. Water would come up to the floorboards of your car and conk out the engine. Getting through the area was nearly impossible. It was especially dangerous because there was a hospital where ambulance access was essential. So, the traffic circle nerds came and did what they had to do and everyone was happy. Except for the people who couldn't drive for shit. They were mad... they were angry and entered the traffic circle backwards and at all the wrong angles until they figured it out. But, eventually everyone was happy. Except it rained and the place flooded like a monsoon again. And everyone got angry again.

So, they had to dig up the circle and lay pipes and underground things that drain the rain away. There's an old carpenter's saying that you "measure twice and cut once," but the engineers of these circles didn't seem to have that philosophy in mind. They went in with a plan and that plan failed, so they constructed the thing again. It only took a hundred years, but eventually they got it right. The circles are amazing. When it rains, it's as dry as the Sahara desert. Everyone rejoiced. Especially those in ambulances. Unless they were dying, then their only concern was not dying.

The engineers and designers also created crosswalks for bikes and pedestrians. Why anyone with sound body and mind would go anywhere near these rotating death traps not encased inside a motored vehicle is beyond me, but I suppose people need to get around in a variety of ways and sometimes those ways are on pedal-powered wheels or on two feet. I once saw an old lady cross the walkway and she looked like a nervous squirrel dashing across a highway. Her fear was palpable. Every car ground to a screeching halt to let her shuffle through the crosswalk, but you could see every driver's obvious impatience. They drummed the steering wheels, gnawed at the steering wheel... gnawed at their wrists, until the lady went through. Then the traffic circle spun like a high-speed blender once again.

I once saw a pack of cyclists go through and I nearly had a coronary. About eight old guys in dick-hugging spandex shorts on their fancy bikes and expensive gear peddled through like a family of clucking ducks. They came through believing everyone would be sensible and respectful of some geezers on their $8,000 bikes and would stop when they entered the crosswalk. But, no. People entering the circle slammed the brakes and honked at them like they were having a picnic in the middle of the road. I thought for sure a Mercedes was going to kill the first biker – his two-wheeled bike replaced with a two-wheeled wheelchair. Another car came zooming through from another angle and almost hit them trying to leave the circle. Suddenly, everyone was yelling at the bikers. The bikers were yelling at them. Words like *disrespect* were being thrown around and of course, someone leaned on their horn so long that it enraged me to the point where I wanted to mow them all down. The circle was backed up for a mile. Cars whirled around, in and out, for about 15 minutes until it was eventually clear and running smooth again.

A few towns over there's a traffic circle with two lanes. Talk about a death trap. If someone is using the inside lane and needs to exit one of the seemingly endless off-shoots that permeate the circle, you can guarantee a series of honks, tire screeches, exaggerated swerves and throat-rattling exchanges will occur out the windows. The main issue with this traffic circle is the size. It's tiny. Way too small for most people and their terrible skills and reaction times. It also has traffic lights, signs and enough road arrows to confuse a map-maker. This nightmare is a major hub of traffic and it's usually a quagmire of craziness that will inflict road rage and anxiety on the most calm and rational driver. Clutter the roundabout with clowns and calliope music and it becomes the twisted carousel of your nightmares. Still, it's safer than the entanglement that was there before, which was a twisted mash of lights and bad signage.

Most issues that plague the sensible traffic circle are the drivers. I'm almost positive I never saw a traffic circle question on my drivers' license exam, but I took my exam way back when Michael Jackson was healing from his first nose job. Maybe today they have traffic circle questions. But, I don't think so. My wife took the exam and I didn't see one traffic circle question. We're simply tossing unsuspecting motorists to the wolves of the world – hoping they'll figure out the whirling, revolving landscape known as the traffic circle.

Of course, we can let people figure it out themselves. But, that's the problem. People are not only stupid, but angry and impatient. They come to a traffic circle and their confusion turns to blind rage. They attack it like most people attack things... with a dull sledgehammer. Unfortunately, that doesn't work with a sensitive and dangerous rotary road such as the traffic circle. Especially since most will be attacking it with a five-ton machine on wheels and the sensitivity of a rhinoceros on methamphetamines, and the patience of a toddler waiting outside a candy store.

The traffic circle is not for the timid, faint-of-heart or the easily rattled. It's not always conducive to the elderly or anyone with poor spacing and timing skills. It's a deathtrap for anyone on a bike or on foot, and it has the potential to be a ramp for daredevils and adrenaline junkies.

And people clamor for flying cars.

Ridiculous.

C'EST LA VIE

I was completely burned out. Mentally exhausted. Fried. I'd been working for almost three years straight without a break and I needed a vacation. The previous year my boss paid me *not* to go on vacation, which was fine because he doubled my salary for two weeks, helping out my anemic savings account, but it did nothing to clear the cobwebs from my mind. This time, I was determined to get away... and not just any old getaway. I was going BIG. I was resolute to leave the country. Steadfast on making plans as complicated as possible; meaning, going to an antiquated New York airport, cramming myself into a miniature airline seat and eating salted nuts until I woke hours later in a country that either spoke a different language, or at the very least, drove on the other side of the road.

After all the mapping and planning and careful assessment of my pitiful bank account, I set a course for adventure to London, England, with a few days in Paris, France for good measure. A dream trip for many. Me for sure. I'd never been to Europe and this was something I could really look forward to. My boss once again tried to buy me out of my vacation, this time *tripling* my salary for the two weeks I'd be gone. But, no amount of money could keep me locked in the cell of an office one more day. It was time to get away.

•••

My flight went off without a hitch… car service to the airport, hopped on a plane and zoom… I was gone. I left New York on a bright sunny April morning and seven hours and multiple bags of salty nuts later, landed in London's Heathrow Airport on a dark evening around 8:00 O'clock. I scheduled a van service into the city, but the van I rented was lost somewhere in the rainy evening and the desk clerk was unable to determine when it would come back… if ever.

So, me and a nice bloke of about 55 named Leslie split a cab into the city. As we drove, Leslie told me a bit about the city and where to go, which all went in one ear and out the other. We talked about Wimbledon, and the Beatles, and any other clichéd British thing I could muster to yap about. Gray-haired and in good shape, Leslie was a well-traveled man and a good sport. We got to his house first, a solid brick standalone with ivy hedges and glowing lanterns, which I could tell was in a very ritzy neighborhood. He paid a sizable portion of the cab fare – enough to cover his part and most of mine – a jolly good showing on his behalf. It was a proper introduction to the hospitable nature of the British.

I arrived at my boutique hotel at 10:00 pm. I rang

the bell and was buzzed in. Dragging my suitcases into the postage stamp lobby, I was greeted by a Czechoslovakian guy who no doubt had rolled out of bed to check me in. His hair matted and sticking up on one side, he looked as if someone had punched him in the nose... a crown of stars circling around his head like a cartoon. My room was a few flights up, a quaint box that looked like every British living room in the country. Dark green walls with dark wood furniture, a TV older than the Queen, and a bathroom similar to one you may find on a 20-foot sailboat.

Because it was 3:00 in the afternoon according to my body clock, I went out for a drink. What no one failed to mention about England was the bars close at something like 7:00 at night, which is the most tragic thing I'd ever heard of in my life. Apparently, if you want to get a few solid hours of drinking in, you've got to start immediately after lunch. I can only assume the quality of work in the offices around the country plummets around noon.

My only avenue to serenity was to go to a dance club a few streets away. I paid 10 Pounds to enter and 2 Pounds for a beer. The conversion rate at the time was a simple One American Dollar to Two Pounds Sterling. Since the British cherish walking around with pockets full of heavy, rattling coins of every conceivable weight and circumference, I took to handing every bartender, merchant and clerk a handful of coins, letting them take what they needed, and handing the rest back. This plan may have lost me a few quid here and there, but in dark, noisy clubs and busy, clanging restaurants, it saved me precious time and much-needed brain cells.

I plopped down on a cushioned cube in the corner

and watched some young kids dance to throbbing beats under disco lighting. I was immediately joined by a disheveled foreigner, who needed an ear to bend. He was distraught because he was desperate for a girlfriend and was struggling to match with anyone in London. I didn't have the heart to tell this Turkish kid that a deafening dance club, while wearing what appeared to be a crooked blue t-shirt he found on his apartment floor, was the last place to make a love connection. So, I simply turned on my New York charm and spouted a series of "you only live once" philosophies. Because I'd been in New York that morning, and London that evening… and most importantly, because I was drinking alcohol, I was suddenly this fascinating man of the world. A sage wizard of advice. A world-traveler and man about town. I told this kid that he needed to have confidence and simply "go for it."

Even though the Turkish lad had a perpetual look on his face of having been punched in the gut, he heeded my call. He stood, yanked his dirty t-shirt and marched over to a girl in a white dress standing with her friends. He talked to her, she smiled and they seemed to be getting along, so I went to the bar to refresh my drink. As the bartender returned my handful of coins, the Turk slid up next to me looking like he'd been punched in the kidneys. Apparently it all went 'London bridges falling down.'

He was appreciative of my zesty "go for it" New York attitude and bought me a shot of vodka. As it rounded midnight, I got the hell out of there before the Turk's depressing funk clung to me and lingered. On my way back to the hotel, I stopped at a burger joint and grabbed a burger to go, even though it was being reported up and down the boulevards that

Hoof and Mouth disease was rampant around the country. It didn't deter me from getting a sloppy deluxe cheeseburger because the burger place was run by Greeks, and I assumed they got their meat from cows that lived by the Mediterranean sea.

In my room I flipped on the TV and watched *Friends*, a show the British seemed to like as well. When that ended, I watched a talk show, then flipped around and watched a puff piece about the obnoxious English band Oasis and before I knew it, it was 4:00 in the morning. I was wide-awake and going to bed was pointless, so I pushed through and grabbed breakfast in the basement cafeteria of the hotel. When I arrived, I was greeted by the waitress/chef, a Czechoslovakian woman who also had the look of someone recently punched in the nose. She made me a traditional English breakfast consisting of eggs, bacon, ham, beans, toast, sheets of lard and the bloody entrails of an animal that bled into a withered tomato. It was four pounds of food meant to jump start my day, but after sitting in my gut for 10 minutes, it induced a coma-like trance that required six or seven cups of coffee to get me back into gear.

Guided under what I can only describe as a jet-lagged, alcohol-tainted high, I wandered around Piccadilly Circus, Leicester and Trafalgar Squares and generally went with the flow -- washing along with currents of people and taking in the sites as I saw fit. I was staying in London for six days, so there was plenty of time to do all the little things I needed to do in good time. The clear, crisp Spring day was ripe for window shopping, looking at old buildings, and catching glimpses of conversations in curt, British tones. By 4:00pm, I was in a tourist trap restaurant, eating a dense Sheppard's pie and falling asleep at the table. I drank a beer, handed the waitress a handful of coins and marched to my hotel, where I proceeded to fall asleep and not awaken until 8:00am the next morning.

•••

My trip planning and research was done completely online, which was convenient in the still fairly early days of the internet. My hotel was located in a posh area known as the Seven Dials section of SOHO, a small square where seven streets converge at a stone sundial pillar. Before I arrived I thought Seven Dials was as infamous as New York's West Village or the Castro District in San Francisco, but every time someone asked me where I was staying, their response to Seven Dials was a variation on:

"Where the bloody hell is that, mate?"

It forced me to point in a general direction, which was usually incorrect, and explain the seven streets and the pillar, until I eventually gave up and told people I was staying near Piccadilly Circus.

Taking advantage of the excellent spring weather, I bought a sandwich and a coffee and spent the entire day atop a blustery double-decker bus tour. I saw just about every square inch of the city as I hopped on and off through the day. I met two girls from Atlanta, took pictures at Buckingham Palace with a German family from Munich, saw Big Ben chime and drank a few beers at a pub with some young business types in suits out on a deck overlooking a square. London has a lot of squares. In fine English manners, I ended the day by passing out with a newspaper filled with fish and chips on my chest while watching the telly.

After my fourth, and last complimentary English breakfast, I headed to Waterloo station where I took a train out to the 'burbs. Back in New York, I'd been seeing an African girl named Mina who moved to London when she was 10. Her father was a melon farmer in Kenya, but gave it up to start a life as an engineer. Mina set me and her family up for dinner at their home in the hamlet of Sidcup. I arrived in the quaint little town with exotic flowers and was greeted warmly -- mainly by the father who needed another man to talk to in a house of four women. When he discovered I loved Jazz music, he poured me fountains of French red wine and DJ'd all his favorite tunes on the record player. Mom made a dinner of chicken with peanut butter sauce, which sounded like something a five year-old threw together, but it's a popular Africa dish and I was pleasantly surprised by the taste.

Mina had two sisters in their late teens, both almost as tall as me. Mina had the most beautiful set of teeth I've ever seen on a human being – a stunning row of white piano keys, the envy of any Hollywood starlet. For some inexplicable reason, Mina's sisters both had mouths filled with, what I can only consider to be a used sets of broken dominos. Not only crooked, their teeth were of varying sizes, jutting out at strange angles and coming in at different lengths. I've heard people chalk up bad British teeth to the amount of sweets they eat, but after seeing three girls cut from the same cloth with completely different sets of choppers, I'm convinced there's something in the English water supply.

After a quick stop at their local recreation center to

drop off snacks for a charity event, the family stuck me on a train zonked on a head full of wine and a small gift of a wood-carved elephant. It would be the last time I ever saw them. Mina and I broke up a few weeks later when she used my phone to make a long distance call to Africa to the tune of $800.

•••

In 1999, I started a world-wide fashion trend that, as of this moment, I still have not received proper credit for. Digging through my father's hall closet one day I came across a rumpled, woolen Irish walking hat. It had hints of Indiana Jones's fedora if you cut the brim really short, constructed it from a beige tweed jacket, crunched it into a ball and left it in my father's hall closet for about 20 years. Because, that's exactly what happened. I pulled this thing out, corked it on my head and sized myself up in the mirror. Not only was I delighted to find it fetching, but the thing had more charm than a pub full of Irish comedians… a personality that rivaled, and even exceeded, my own.

Starting in the Fall of 1998, I wore this charming, rumpled tweed hat religiously. Everywhere I went I receiving nothing but praise and outright compliments from every person who saw me. I was approached daily in the streets by strangers who'd tell me they loved the hat. Patrons in bars would haggle to buy it from me outright, fanning large bills in my face like tempting seductresses. Every man wanted to know where I bought it and every woman wanted it for the man in their life. I was basically a rock star. Without the hat

I was nobody... wallpaper in the endless background of New York. But *with* the hat, people would truck over fashion models and minor celebrities to admit their envy in my ownership of the hat.

And I'm not talking about Pharrell Williams and his drunken "man in the yellow hat" cowboy shenanigans, who looked like a large caliber bullet to be chambered into a rifle and shot at a charging rhino. My hat was iconic in its stylish wear-ability, but also in its functionality. It repelled the rain like a turtle shell; was warm like a fuzzy mink coat, and not only did it need no care whatsoever, it almost required that I roll it into a ball and toss it on the floor. Neglect was how it was born into greatness and neglect was what it loved and needed.

Four months later, as sure as the sun rises over the East River, every fucking asshole in Manhattan was wearing my exact hat in the cool spring air. Literally everyone. Every man, every woman, every child and every celebrity you saw in every tabloid rag was donning my fantastic rumpled walking hat. Some were exact replicas, some were slightly off but still had the same "feeling" as my hat, and some missed the mark completely in charm and style, as well as functionality. It was infuriating because my hat was an original formed in fire... or, in the darkened closet of decades past. It couldn't be matched by the finest designers and milliners in the entire world.

My hat, which at one point was the most original in all of New York was now a dime a dozen. Walking the Manhattan streets of SOHO and the West Village garnered me no esteem, no double looks, and I was certainly not offered any treasures for the hat's acquisition. In fact if anything, it was a cliché. Where before I was an original, I was now in lock-step with the other posers of the world and their temporary, rumpled-hat fashion statement that would die like a pot of daffodils once the Summer heat beat down on our heads.

Two years later, I tried to resurrect this stunning rumpled hat fashion statement in London on my grand trip around the city because, as was to be expected during a London spring, the skies opened and the rain crashed down in sheets. Since I'd already hit all the museums on a sunny day, I walked around in my hat, went to a movie theater and pub-hopped on my way back to the hotel. Not only did my rumpled Irish tweed hat leave little impression, it was outright mocked by the British. I thought a tweed hat of this nature was a rite of passage… something most people had within arms-reach in the moistest part of the world. Ireland is right next door to the freakin' country. The Irish are everywhere. But nope… my hat didn't make an impression. While walking early in the rainy day, two blokes muttered under their breath:

"Nice cap, mate."

"Yea, really nice cap, mate."

Their sarcasm was so extreme I practically needed a squeegee to clean it off.

I was prepared to turn and defend my hat, but I'm not one to enter fisticuffs over headwear in a foreign country. The last thing I needed was to get tossed in the clink in a city where they barely speak English. My case of *Man vs. Hat* would be defended by a barrister wearing a hat of white rat hair – something George Washington wore on his head when he kicked the ass of the country I was currently in, during the glorious year of 1776.

So I zipped my mouth shut and slunk around in my terribly unpopular hat. At that point I was stuck with it. I couldn't take it off as it was raining buckets. Every pub I entered I was met by a meaty bartender who looked at my head like I was wearing a live beaver. Then, eventually, they looked into my eyes with confusion and displaced shame. After the bartenders returned my handful of coins accompanied by a pint, they'd ignore me so I could drink alone with my wet hat. No women were interested in me and no one found me fashionable or trendy. It was a cold, dark world where New York fashion hadn't made it across the pond, nor did it seem like it ever would.

Fortunately, the next day, I would be going someplace where fashion was not only alive and well, but where fashion was practically invented... Paris, France.

•••

There's a small rumor going around that the French don't like Americans all that much. They're adverse to people prancing through their country like John Wayne, acting like they have church bells for balls and proclaiming that if it wasn't for the good, old US of A, France would be a pile of rubble and speaking German. Of course, the Good Old US of A would be bowing to a English king if it wasn't for France because they saved our asses during the American Revolution, but that kind of history has been lost on most Americans because... well... they're Americans, educated in the American schooling system. Not only that, any history that didn't happen in the last 100 years or so is lost in time. So, I was both excited and apprehensive about going to Paris. How would I be treated? Who are the French? Have I been brainwashed by TV and film? Or is it as bad as everyone says?

I awoke early on a Thursday and went to the St. Pancras International station, a charming, white-pillared station filled with shops and small cafés. I hopped on the Eurostar train to Paris at about 10:00am, having purchased a very expensive ticket a few days before. The train shot me out of the station and into the lush, green country side of England – its rolling hills and misty moors zipping by my window as the rainy haze lifted, giving way to some sun. I had the whole row to myself on a rather empty train. Across the aisle, a gorgeous blonde Frenchwoman, athletic and wearing a stylish fitness outfit costing more than my entire wardrobe, yapped on her cell phone for the entire two and a half hour trip. Her clothes were so chic and polished, I swear she was from the future.

As the view outside my window crossed from thick, leafy hills and valleys, to a dark Chunnel crossing, then to flat, desert terrain pocked with thin sycamore trees, I tucked my fashionable, rumpled hat into my small bag and retired my brown leather coat for the duration of my French excursion. My plan was to spend three days in Paris, then return to the Seven Dial Hotel, where they were holding my large suitcase, allowing me to travel with a simple carry-on bag.

Because I live for adventure, or as one could say, I like to "wing it" and NOT because I'm a dumbass, I went to Paris without a hotel reservation of any kind. So not only was I taking a train to a foreign country that I'd never been to, where the people could potentially not talk to me, or even understand me, and have a reputation for *hating* people like me, I was planning on randomly showing up and figuring it out as I went. A plan I now think about in hindsight, was stupid enough to give the average person an anxiety attack. My one saving grace, was a small sheet of paper that Mina had given me with about 20 French terms I could use in a pinch if necessary. Things like "Bonne Journee" – Good Day; "Bonsoir" – Good Evening; "Bonne Nuit" – Good Night; and the ever critical, "j'ai besoin de la police" – I need the police.

Mina also told me that her French friends "may" come and meet me to help the poor American out, but after 15 minutes in Paris's airy and majestic Gare du Nord station platform, a place that could rival any train station in the world for its noisy, bombast of chaos, I knew I was very much on my own. That notion was solidified when I picked up the pay phone to call Mina's friend and the female operator berated me for not understanding the telephone system. Like England, I was accustomed to someone handing me change in return for my purchase, but when I stuffed some random coins into the soulless phone slot, hoping it would prompt some kind of ring tone, the operator barked at me in broken English and the line went dead.

Fortunately at that time, the French Franc was garbage and my American money garnered me a treasure trove of cash. I swapped money at the exchange window and got on line for a taxi. Once inside the cab, I tried to explain to my driver that I didn't have a destination and needed a hotel. After we shot out of the station like a cannonball, I continued to explain to my dark-skinned cabbie that I needed a hotel and there was no destination. Unfortunately, not only did my Pakistani driver not understand English at a high level, He didn't understand French at a high level either. I shouted into the back of his head a half dozen times that I NEEDED a hotel, which finally registered and he excitedly took me to a small boutique hotel near the river, right on the corner of a quaint little street. A hotel run by "his friends." He dropped me off, sped away and I went to the hotel. The doors were locked. On close inspection, they were out of business. The lobby was a wash of dull white paint and in various forms of neglect. I spun around and a homeless Frenchman laughed at me in a smug and mocking way. I wasn't in the position to mock him back, so I barreled forward, dragging my little suitcase behind me to a main avenue.

I held out my hand and a cab screamed to a halt... I mean, smoke coming from the tires and everything. The passenger window rolled down and the woman manning the cab shouted "where are you going?" She marked me as a desperate and stupid American in about two seconds. I said "The hotel I was staying closed down" and pointed incredulously to the empty boutique behind me.

"Get in!" she shouted, and I hopped in the backseat like a bank heist.

She floored the car, ashed her cigarette out the window and accessed the situation.

"You say the hotel your reserved closed and you need a hotel?"

"Thant's right." I said with partial truth.

"No problem!"

All of five foot two with hair like straw, this 40 year-old firecracker hit turns going 100 kilometers per second as easily as taking in a lung full of smoke. This fabulous French-woman pulled out a map and laid it on the steering like it was the drafting table in a war room. She was stabbing the map, noting areas of interest and asking me questions while avoiding pedestrians like a Hollywood stunt driver. What drugs she was on, I'm not sure, but I was willing to follow this woman to the ends of the earth – no questions asked.

Eventually, by luck or by chance, we came to a modest hotel on some nameless street in the Latin Quarter. She told me to run in and see if they had a room, which according to the young female desk clerk, they did. For a mere 200 Francs, an easily digestible 30 bucks in US dollars, I could have a seventh floor walkup room with a shared bathroom. I pounced on the deal. I thanked my superstar cabbie, who waved and shouted "Welcome to Paris!" as she streamed down the Rue like a comet into the twilight.

I settled into my muted pink-walled room, which smelled like moldy tobacco and 500 years of French history. I flung open the barn door windows and settled into the small wooden desk in front of it, smoking American Spirit cigarettes and contemplating life while staring over the decrepit slate rooftops that caught the light of the falling sun. Not only was I in Paris, but, I was suddenly French by proxy. I felt my inner monologue become more laissez-faire, the stress of the world's problems becoming the problems of anyone but me and my French compatriots. In my creamy-papered journal, I wrote inspired passages, notes of travelogue, and clever doodles as I gazed onto the street below, chain-smoking, and wondering why François Truffaut wasn't a superstar in the eyes of America. My journal passages would become fodder for future films – all shot in stark black and white and starring people with dark-circled eyes who have brown cigarettes permanently glued to their lips. The French love to smoke. Every café you pass, someone has a thick cloud forming around their head. I believe the reason Godard called his famous film *Breathless* was because no one had any lung capacity.

Hunger eventually took over, so I hit the streets. I went right across the street to a bar, but was informed after chugging an orange juice that they didn't serve food. Down a main avenue, I entered a bistro and was commanded by the bar maid to "sit down" which I did like a scolded schoolboy. Taking a fabulous window seat, I ate duck l'orange as the misty day turned into a purple night. I was fed beers by the barmaid, who could easily bench press me after she'd worked a double shift. She sent me off with a smile and a belly so full of rich French food and beer that I almost called a cab to take me the 300 meters I needed to travel back to my room. I collapsed in my squishy bed, unbathed and reeking of duck, cigarettes, and everything that make French life enviable to all those around the globe who know it through romantic films and slick fashion magazines.

•••

There's a phenomenon called Paris Syndrome. Apparently some people who visit the City of Lights are overcome with a form of Psychosis. Symptoms can include anxiety, paranoia, hallucinations and even vomiting. Affecting mainly Japanese and Chinese tourists, it's been known to affect other visitors as well. Some experts think the cause of this phenomena is a form of culture shock – a realization that the glamorous and cosmopolitan city they've seen in films and TV is actually a dirty, claustrophobic nightmare filled with rude and callous bums. I'd like to think this phenomenon occurs because the city is built on a pet cemetery or on a strange magnetic field – or perhaps it's the gateway to hell, requiring the priests in the multiple gothic churches around the city to be in a constant state of exorcism.

Whatever the feeling is, I found the city to be EXACTLY how I saw it in film and TV – every expectation met. The city was gorgeous, packed with charming stores and cafés, engraved with gnarly Art Nouveu design and towering with historic architectural features inlaid into every buildings and flowing fountain. The only expectation that had not been met thus far was my encounter with the terrible, rude French that is imbedded into the mindset of the world. Sure, I'd encountered some aloofness... maybe even some apathy... but outright rudeness? Not at all. But that was all about to change.

The next morning I hit the streets with a renewed vigor. I saw the Eiffel Tower in the distance and walked towards it – my destination for the day – about three kilometers away. It was a stunning day. Not a cloud in the sky. I passed a large open café and decided to have some breakfast. I entered and was met by an elderly maître d', who I greeted with a convincing "Bonjour" who sat me down and rattled off a stream of French words that locked me into a state of panic. I accepted a menu and sheepishly said, "Sorry, I don't speak French." Well, let me tell you, his bright smile fell to a deep frown so severe, I thought he might strike me. Apparently my

"Bonjour" greeting was so convincing, he pegged me for a Frenchman. I'm not sure why. Perhaps because I'd failed to bring electric outlet converters for my electric razor, I was going on two weeks without a shave and was looking scrappy. I was staying in a building with a shared bathroom and I was a few days unshowered. And I was wearing a beat up brown short coat that was both fashionable, yet also stuck it's thumb in the eye of convention as it wasn't appropriate for the warm summer-like weather in the air. So my immersion into the French mystique was complete. Perhaps to a fault. The maître d', feeling duped, stormed off and that was that. He never came back... and it was clear that he told the rest of the staff to ignore me as well, because the other waiters sat, and served other customers while I looked around like a lost puppy. Cleary the waiters did not agree with the boss about ignoring me and shot me passing sympathetic glances while I waited like an idiot for service. Even the other customers noted my lack of food or attention. A waiter went to his boss and pleaded to serve me but I saw him waved off – the waiter walking away frustrated, knowing his job was on the line. Finally after about 15 minutes, I stood with my tail between my legs and departed, holding out my hands, shaking my head and pantomiming a display of hurt and confusion. All I got was 20 pairs of eyes staring at me as I continued down the boulevard towards the Eiffel tower.

That was it. That was my "welcome to the French" moment. Not a cool slight, murmured under a breath...or an outward look of disgust. This was a toss into the cold, deep end of the pool. As much indignation as one could get in a simple pedestrian experience. I have to say, it was one of the toughest moments I ever had in my life. The walk to the exit of the café felt like it took a small eternity. And once I was off again, strolling down the boulevard, my heart grew cold. I went from doe-eyed babe, to a man watching his back. I saw every person as a potential threat and every business a potential landmine. I didn't fall into a state of hallucination and vomit, but it was a culture shock to be sure. Every terrible French cliché punched me in the face in that moment and now my expectations of Paris were fulfilled completely.

After navigating through some side streets, I came to the Eiffel Tower garden and immediately hit a snack kiosk near the tower. Approaching tentatively, I scanned the limited menu, taking my time to order what I wanted while also going over in my mind how to pronounce my item correctly. I was starving and couldn't handle another food rejection. I smiled weakly and stated my order to the skinny blond teenage girl leaning above me at the counter.

"Eh, Bonjour. Un Jambon et Fromag…

"We speak English here!" she barked like a truck-stop waitress from Pennsylvania. "You want a ham and cheese bagette?"

"Yes, please." I said shrinking.

What she really wanted to say was "you want a ham and cheese baguette, you dumb fucking American sheep who I see 500 times a day in this god-forsaken place?" but she held back her words, her attitude doing the speaking for her. She slammed the sandwich down and asked for 35 Francs, which I gladly paid. I sat at a small table and inhaled the sandwich like oxygen.

I bought a ticket to the Eiffel Tower and went up... at first on the lower tier and then to the top. I stayed up there for an hour. It was amazing. Beautiful sunshine, light breeze, stunning city views and no French to yell at me. A singular, visceral moment I won't forget in my lifetime. The French probably feel about the Eiffel Tower how I feel about the Empire State Building... a tall thing in the middle of my city. But it's truly an amazing monument and worthy of a visit.

Later, I hopped on a bus tour and did a big loop, capturing all the major structures. Upon my return to the beginning of the bus loop, I went to the sandwich kiosk and purchased two more Jambon et Fromage sandwich baguettes, one I ate immediately and one I stuffed in my pocket for dinner. Still shell-shocked from breakfast, I wasn't sure I could handle a restaurant visit in the evening, so a pocket ham sandwich was a good emergency bite to eat. I walked to the Notre Dame Cathedral, past the Pantheon and then to my hotel. Entering the place, I passed a new desk clerk, a dark-haired woman of about 50 who looked at me as if a tumbleweed rolled into her lobby. I sang "Bon Soir" and walked up to my room.

I sat at my desk, prepared to write deep, meaningful passages into my journal, and sink a bite into my sandwich when the phone rang. I picked it up and said a cautious "hello." It was a man.

"Yez, hallo. Is this Mr. Schmitz?"

"Yes it is." I said cautiously.

"Zis iz the manager. I'm afraid we've made a mistake and you will need to check out tomorrow."

"Tomorrow?" I said swallowing my bite.

"Yez, sir. Az you see, we've made a mistake and the

room is taken for the next few days. All the rooms are taken. You understand, yes?"

"Yes."

"Thank you for understanding. Bon Noie."

Deflated, I wrapped my sandwich, put on my coat and headed out the door. Passing the clerk, I gave a snide smirk and walked down the street. Within seconds I was on Rue Monge, a quaint road filled with hotels. I bopped into the first place I saw and asked the desk manager if they had any rooms available for the next few days. With a mound of black, slicked-back hair and pencil-thin moustache, He looked at me like my dick was hanging from my zipper.

"No. We have no rooms for YOU! What kind of place do you think this is?"

"It looks like a hotel."

"Yes, of course it's a hotel. But you need to have a reservation to stay here. We don't let anyone walk off the street to stay here! Do you understand this?"

"I do now. Thank you."

I turned and walked away from the clerk, who clacked a last indignant huff with some accompanying French, which according to my natural "Angry foreign language to English translator" converted his words to "These ugly Americans and their desire to be accommodated! Simply awful!"

I walked a few meters down Rue Monge and came to another place and approached the clerk.

"Do you have any rooms available for tomorrow night and the following evening?"

The thin, blonde clerk looked up at me and smiled, his eyes sparkling like diamonds in the sky. This was exactly the man I needed... as gay as Gay Par-ee can get. He flipped open the reservation book, ran his finger down the ledger and nodded.

"Yes," he said in a soft voice, "We do. A few rooms. Shall I reserve one for you?"

"Yes, please." I said enthusiastically.

I explained that I was being kicked out of my other hotel.

"Since you are leaving your other room, would you prefer an early check in tomorrow?"

"That would be amazing!" I beamed.

"7:00 AM okay for you?"

"Perfect."

He rang the bill, I paid, and within 20 minutes of being ejected from my old room, I had another. I thanked him for his kindness and he smiled like I was a movie star.

"We look forward to having you."

I was so happy to snag another hotel quickly, in my joy, I strolled to the Pantheon area and had dinner at an Italian restaurant. The host was nice enough, and sat me quickly. The menu was in Italian and the prices were still in Liras, which Italy had replaced with the Euro a few years before, but I paid it no mind. My waiter had to translate the choices in very rough English, but he suggested a bowl of Ragu alla Bolognese with tagliatelle noodles, which I scarfed down like water. I had a few glasses of red wine and left buzzed and airy.

When I received my credit card bill a month later, after all the ridiculous conversions of Liras to Francs to Euros to Dollars, my tiny bowl of pasta and two watered down glasses of cheap table wine cost me $140. C'est la vie.

The next day I dragged my suitcase a few blocks to my new hotel. Unlike the sweet guy from the night before, I was greeted by a man who, much like the clerk who rejected me a few doors down, recoiled in terror at the sight of me. Again, sizing me up and down as if I had my testicles draped out of my zipper, he frowned as I came to him face to face.

"Checking in... Schmitz." I said politely, but with a bit of an edge.

At this point, I was tired, a touch ragged, and feeling a little defiant. I'd not showered in days and my meals were coming in fits of pick-pocket opportunity.

"Yes, Schmitz." he dripped. "You're lucky to have a room here. I'm not sure why Victor gave you a room, we are so booked."

"You seemed to have multiple vacancies last night." I snapped.

"Yes, but there are many people coming. I have no choice but to honor the room seeing as you've already paid."

"Yes. Thank you." I said, kindly agreeing with his position.

I accepted my room key and took the elevator up. I was beginning to think I wasn't welcome in Paris. But I couldn't be the only one afflicted by this. There seemed to be a systematic plan to un-room and board people... reservations be damned. I thought the point of a hotel was to accommodate guests but these clerks seemed determined to hinder that by making it seem ridiculous to even ask if there's a room to shelter in.

At this point, Paris Syndrome didn't seem like much of a phenomenon at all... this mysterious "syndrome" where people felt strange, disillusioned and anxious because of Paris. Evidence pointed to the outright fact most Parisians were being fucking assholes – outwardly hostile to the point of being dangerous. Aggressively ugly... every response and statement shot with poisonous venom. Yes, we have some ugly Americans, guilty of superiority and wearing socks with sandals. But what I was experiencing was something far more sinister. A systematic desire to be ungodly nasty... a comeuppance for past transgressions to be paid in full with a fiery scorn displaced onto the soul of every visitor to roam the Parisian streets. Maybe even Shadenfeude. I was baffled. The nasty reputation of the French wasn't just alive and well – it was monstrous!

My room, of course, was right next to the elevator. The sound of the lift whooshing through the wall was so evident, I could hear the gears cranking and the cables extending and resting on top of the car with each pass up and down. My bathroom was bright and clean, but there was no shower -- only an old claw-foot tub with a shower faucet nozzle, which didn't go more than three feet high. I showered on my knees in a ball, the lukewarm water spitting on me like a drinking fountain. I believe washing with an electric toothbrush would have been more effective.

•••

I attacked the new day with a fresh enthusiasm. I headed directly to the Louvre Museum, where I ate crepes and coffee at a café nearby where I was waited on, but not by anyone who was happy to serve me.

Once inside the glass pyramid and into the belly of

the Louvre, I roamed free without care as history unfolded before my eyes. Pudgy cherub women danced in gardens inside gilded frames as tall as a house; Egyptian artifacts, the envy of every swashbuckling adventurer to dig the earth, glinted in the sun; and a few million marble statues came at me in armies of glowing white. The Mona Lisa was extremely small... hardly viewable as I couldn't get more than 10 feet from her with the small mob encircling it like a rock star. I stumbled upon the statue of Venus de Milo, which was taller than I thought she would be.

She was discovered by a Greek farmer, buried in city ruins on the island of Milos. Both of her arms were missing, but small pieces of hand and arm were in tact nearby that indicate she was holding an apple. Artists and sculptors have tried to replicate what her arms may have actually been doing... some showing her leaning on a pillar with an apple, some showing her with arms raised like she was playing an instrument or holding a chain. I believe, with no proof whatsoever, that she had the fingers on her right arm touching her labia, and the fingers of her left arm touching her butthole. Back in the day, this caused some prude to fly into a rage at the pornographic scene, knock her arms off with a hammer, and dump Venus into a hole. This theory is based on nothing, with no art history knowledge of the statue and nothing other than my perverted mind to create a strange, yet plausible scenario. I'm not sure if this hypothesis has been entered into the rationale, but consider this my submission.

I spent the entire day in the museum, eating a ham and cheese baguette around lunchtime in the cafeteria. I was served at the counter by a woman in black leather, who looked as if she was dressed to eat at a fine restaurant and not handing out café sandwiches to obnoxious Americans. Again, I was served with the attitude of someone who'd asked for a kidney donation and not a meat and cheese sandwich. I considered ordering another sandwich for my pocket, but I was tired of pocket food. I wanted to sit in a restaurant. Besides, at that point, the leather-clad woman had clacked away on her high-heels to yell at an assistant shelving quiches into a case.

Outside again, I sat in a folded chair next to the Grand Bassin Rond, a large fountain that spritzed water into the air and refreshed my face. I watched a child foil a juggler, and nodded off as the sun began to fall.

At this point I was pretty beat. I'd been traveling for almost 10 days without break and I was worn. While passing by the Greek restaurant across the street from my hotel, I noticed a sign in the window that stated *Americans Welcome*, a huge relief and a window into the soul of the city. I was seated at a table by a balding waiter who hit me with such clear, harshly projected English, that if the window sign hadn't existed, I would have thought I wasn't welcome at all.

Within minutes I was chatting with a tall, dark-haired American named Chris from San Diego across the small restaurant. The waiter too snuck in and out of the conversation and it was a nice chat. Chris had just landed and was staying in the same hotel. He asked me if there were lots of places to get a drink. I said confidently, that you could get a drink on literally ever corner, which is true. I also said "you can get a beer in a McDonald's, and I mean a glass of beer" referencing the line from the film *Pulp Fiction*, which went over everyone's head, even though it was like the most famous film in history at that point and even won the fucking Palme D'or, the highest honor at Cannes film festival, which is in France, by the way… a stone's throw away from where we were sitting. I chalked it up as a lost cause and didn't reference my food as being better than a Royal with Cheese.

Chris told me he flew in with an Irish guy who suggested meeting him later at an American bar where they spoke English and played American sports on TV. We finished eating, refreshed ourselves and hit the street as the night came.

There's a fantastic episode of *The Simpsons* from Season 1 where Bart goes to France as an exchange student. He becomes a slave to criminal wine makers who plan to sell altered wine using antifreeze. Bart is sent to the store to buy it, but can't communicate with the shopkeeper in English. As he walks away frustrated, he curses himself in French and realizes he's able to speak it fluently. Shockingly, I experienced the same thing. As Chris and I wandered the streets looking for the bar, I approached a beat cop in a yellow vest. Referencing my notes, I approached him and he smiled warmly at me and said "Bonjoir." I returned a "Bonjour" but realized it was night and correctly said, "Bon Soir" and pointed to the night sky. The policeman laughed and said "Bon Soir." Before I knew it I was speaking in clear French, asking him where I could find the bar. He pointed and told me the location and I understood it almost completely. It was amazing. Like a switch flipped in my head. Not only that, I was doing it unconsciously… like I was listening to someone else.

We found the place and immediately approached the bar. I spoke to the bartender in French and a dark, curly-haired guy in an Allen Iverson Philadelphia 76ers jersey said, "They speak English here!" which snapped me out of my French-speaking immersion. We ordered two beers, drank, and exchanged hometowns with the other Americans in the bar. The Irishman eventually showed – a heavy-set, tight-curled strawberry blonde chap named Brian who rolled in like a party animal. He knew the crowd and we all knocked back shots of Jameson.

Chris suddenly didn't feel well and dropped out.

"I think I'm jet-lagged." He said spinning away from the bar. I never saw him again.

Brian and I drank more, then he suggested we go to a club. We hopped in a taxi and while cruising through the streets, he talked on his cell phone in French. Again, my sudden clarity in the language helped me comprehend. It was clear through the conversation that Brian was a gay man, trying to hook up with unsuspecting Americans by playing the nice tourist-trap guide, helping a fellow English speaker by being a friendly face in the crowd.

"You speak French?" He asked when I turned to examine his face.

"Not a word." I said.

He smiled and continued his conversation, throwing his head back like a fat cat about to eat the canary.

At the club, Brian paid for us to get in… a chic club that was very high class. He ordered champagne at the bar. We sipped from fizzy flutes, then hit the dance floor, chatting up cute French girls when my head began to swim. I excused myself and went downstairs. I got my coat I checked at the door, and the next thing I knew I was waking up on the front stoop of the club, a doorman kicking the bottom of my foot asking:

"Hos-Pi-Tal? Hey! Hos-Pi-Tal?"

I don't know if I passed out or blacked out, but all I could muster at the time was a simple "taxi."
They lifted me up, tossed me in the back of a cab and the driver asked me, "Where to?"

"Rue Monge" I said, and he drove.

In French, the driver was asking me questions, which I could understand, but my only response was "Rue Monge" which he replied to with a nod. I saw my hotel and pointed.

I went to my room and fell asleep and didn't wake until 11:00am the next morning when the obnoxious French phone rang off the hook. I answered to the snobby clerk.

"Mr. Schmitz, you must leave ze room today for cleaning service."

"I don't want cleaning service." I said with a misty head.

"But sir, you must vacate the premises for the day. We MUST clean the room."

"I don't want to leave." I begged. "I don't feel well. I think I'm coming down with a cold."

That was the truth. I'm not sure if Brian had put something in my drink or what... Chris did bail early not feeling well, and I had something come over me quickly in the club, but I was definitely getting sick. My nose was clogged and I was under the weather.

"Please, you must go and you can return at three."

"Fine!" I yelled into the phone, and slammed it down. Stomping through the lobby, the clerk signaled to talk to me, but I blew past and stormed out the door. I was officially done with the French and their bullshit. I needed headache medicine, but because the French enjoy taking four-hour lunches, I wandered the street looking for any business to be open so I could get some kind of pain relief. Eventually I came to the only place I could find open, and that was a small Chinese restaurant café. I walked in and pointed to a bunch of stuff in a glass case. The Chinese woman behind the counter didn't speak one word to me, didn't smile, and may actually have been a robot. She served me at the one tiny table against the wall, including a bowl of warm Miso soup, and within minutes I was back on track.

I walked along the Seine River and watched the boats drift by, bent over the shoulders of artists who were oil painting on their easels, and browsed the books and postcards of sellers displaying their authentic wares through endless rows of towering, makeshift, old-fashioned library stands. By that point, I was officially done -- with traveling and with Paris. By the evening I was in full nose-cold mode. I stopped by the Chinese place and grabbed food to go and ate it in my room.

In the morning, I tossed my room card at the terrible clerk and left without a word. He tried to settle up my minibar bill... the one orange juice I swigged the previous morning, but I walked away before he could finish his sentence. I stuck my hand out and was in a cab in seconds, back to the Gare du Nord station, which, upon my initial arrival was a glass dome of intrigue, but was now a greenhouse of noxious gas that sent me off in a state of stale funk.

Out of the Chunnel on the English side, I felt a tremendous sense of relief to find the rolling English hills and damp mist to greet me. My rumpled hat had not been accepted in London, but it wouldn't deter me from wearing it in the damp, cool spring air that still lingered when I left a few days before.

The French and English did not get along… that much was clear. I wasn't exactly in lock-step with the British myself, but we stood on common ground. We both found the French to be an intolerable group of misanthropes, incurable in their hatred for everyone outside their country, and maybe hatred for everyone in their country as well, including their own reflections in the mirror.

Still, there is a lot to love about Paris. It's a beautiful city… packed with history and intrigue. Through my adventures I found most of the blue-collar people to not only be polite, but upstanding. Hotel clerks, waiters and those in the customer service business? Simply dreadful.

Where did it all go wrong? When did the Franco-American relationship fall apart? During the American Revolution, George Washington heaped nothing but praise on the French, calling Lafayette, the inspired revolutionary Frenchman "like a son to me." Our beloved forefather Benjamin Franklin spent years in France, finding the French not only fun and decadent, but well-educated and of a higher standard. Ben banged the powdered and perfumed hussies of the upper crust, never wanting to return to the US until John Adams begged him to bring his fat, wine-soaked ass back home to fulfill his duty as a pillar of our country.

During the French Revolution, America kept its mouth shut… and during the American Civil War, the French kept their mouth shut. Then Hilter marched over half of Europe and we sent half a million men to die on the world's beaches in the ultimate cause to liberate the oppressed and save the planet. Everything seemed to be going fine.

We thought our continued dislike of Russia, sanctions on a Mussolini-hungover Italy and broken Germany, as well as a watchful eye on every other land-snatching super power, would keep America and France in good graces for a long time. But, something happened along the way. Maybe it was the cold war, or maybe France wasn't invited to the table when all the king's horses and all the king's men put Europe back together again. But the slow, cold decent into a cold shoulder for the USA, England, and other thoughtful and kind neighbors has perplexed the planet for nearly a century.

The French have a long history of great artistic individuality... of original, simplistic flair, free of excess. Compared to garish Americans and their narcissistic vulgarity and flaunting wealth, the French were the idealist earth dweller. Unencumbered by class systems and repelled by the endless churning of the money system, the French lived the sweet life... well rested, well fed and not driven by the senseless grind of work. While the USA was killing themselves for the biggest and the best stuff, the French sat back and enjoyed everything they had. As time went on, the divide became greater.

But, we're only products of the people who came before us. Unfortunately, the relationship seems irrevocably broken. I've been told that the French are great, and I only need to be around the *right* people. I'm sure that is true on some level, but for me to achieve that introduction, I would need to make the effort on my part... a resolution I do not plan to undertake anytime soon.

Like a Tiffany vase filled with rotten, squirming worms, I am left to remember only a beautiful, artistic city filled with snapping, venomous snakes.

•••

I checked back into the Seven Dials hotel again, worn and nursing a head cold. When I inquired about my suitcase, the young Czech pulled it out from under the counter like he was using it as a chair. I checked into another room... this time two flights higher than my previous room and twice as dark as it faced the back of the building – looking over a dank alley. I drank tea and watched TV all day, getting myself right, and ended the day with a burger down the street, continuing my pursuit of catching Hoof and Mouth diseases with every bite.

The next day I wandered the streets and shopped, purchasing a pair of leather shoes and gifts for the folks back home. When I got back to the hotel, I had a message from Mina's sister Veronica who wanted to know if I was interested in dancing with her and a friend at some clubs. I called her back and said yes, even though I was functioning at 50 percent.

Even though Mina was a manageable 5' 4", her sister Veronica was a gargantuan six feet tall, and towered over me in her stiletto heels when I met her at the train station. She was dressed in a cute purple cocktail dress and her friend, standing a foot shorter than her, was stuffed like a sausage in what I could only determine was a pink and orange water balloon – her chubby rolls of fat bulging like pizza dough at every conceivable location of her body. We started by drinking beer at an outdoor café near Piccadilly Circus and after some light banter, I came to a realization that my drinking mates may have been a tad younger than me. When I asked their age, Veronica told me she was 17 and her friend 16. Not only was I carousing with underage girls on foreign territory, I was feeding them alcohol. England's drinking age is 18, and Veronica could easily pass for 20, but her sausage smuggling friend didn't look a day over 15 and the more I examined her, the worse it got. He face was smeared with thick makeup – like a child who'd gotten into mommy's beauty case after attacking her sister's closet – sheathing herself in a dress meant for someone half her size. Like Mina, Veronica had dark chocolate complexion, but her friend was mixed race, her skin a muted tan, which was evident by the off-white foundation she pancaked in a circle over her face like a circus clown. Her aqua eye-shadow was paired with screaming pink lipstick that she was unable to keep within her actual lip line, frustrating every anal-retentive coloring book artist far and wide. It all made for a twisted horror show. It was clear this was her first night out on the town and I was lucky enough to be the chaperone for this fashion mistake. I know we were in Piccadilly Circus, but this was ridiculous.

Eventually the three of us made it to a thumping club, but I was denied entry because I was wearing "trainers." I couldn't understand what the hell the guy was mumbling about and Veronica translated into ENGLISH English that I was wearing sneakers. My immediate thought was "they call sneakers: trainers? What a stupid name." Then I realized that in America, we call sneakers SNEAKERS, and the more I thought about *that*, the more I realized how incredibly stupid the name sneakers is. The British must think we're morons, sneaking around in our sneakers. What are we? Cat burglars? Silently shifting around in our everyday life, avoiding sound... getting in and out before we're caught red-handed?

Fortunately we were close to the hotel. I brought the girls up to the room and I shoe-horned my new, stiff leather shoes onto my feet when the phone rang. It was the young Czech desk clerk who informed me I was not to have any "guests" in my room. I assumed he meant whores, and judging from Veronica's friend, I got the impression that's what he thought. But I told him I was changing from trainers to shoes so we could go dancing.

We danced and drank vodka tonics and to my surprise, I ran into the downtrodden Turkish man I'd met the night of my arrival. He didn't recognize me at all. He again confessed his need to be paired with a girl and although I was tempted to throw Veronica's friend at him, I had mercy on them both. I told him good luck and walked away. From the looks of him, his issues were more about heavy drinking in loud dance clubs and less about finding a quality love connection. I put the girls on a train back home and never saw them again.

•••

On my flight back to New York, I sat next to a guy named John, who went by Buster, and his sister Cara at the window seat. About half an hour before landing, we started chatting and before long, I was giving Buster my phone number. He called a few days later and I took him and Cara out on an East Village drinking tour. Starting at McSorley's Ale House, we marched around the village late into the night until we found ourselves at a small Jazz club on 13th street, tucked into couches drinking hard liquor. Cara informed me she was 18, continuing my spree of feeding underage girls alcohol, endangering my good name and my legal standing within the community. Fortunately I was back on my own soil, prepared to deal with any legal issues with people who spoke clear, admissible English in an accent that didn't sound like it was said with a mouthful of marbles or shot at me with a snobby cobra's poisonous snap.

Back at work, I mentally prepared for my next big trip. Where would I go? My list of foreign countries to wander through ran long, but my pockets, unfortunately, were not deep. Japan? Australia? Germany? The world was my oyster. But, because I'm an American, functioning under the traditional system of never-ending work... grinding away... avoiding the appearance of being lazy, entitled and weak, or simply motivated by the fear of being swallowed by the hungry beast known as bills and rent, I did not go on vacation, on foreign or U.S. soil, for another three, long years.

BLONDE ON BLONDE

What did the blonde order at the bar?

A beer.

That's it! Just a beer. There's no joke here! How dare you think this was a setup for a blonde joke. Who do you think you are? Why are there blonde jokes? I'm blonde and pretty intelligent... I think. I went to summer school three times, but that has more to do with my terrible attention span than anything else. I have the attention span of a goldfish. Tell me something interesting and I'll immediately forget it. But, with the passage of time and proper fermenting, that nugget of information will spring out when least expected. Usually while I'm washing the patio furniture, or once in a great while – on a rare occasion – when I'm playing *Trivial Pursuit* and it actually benefits my team. My brain is like my office cabinet... loaded with stuff that is completely unorganized.

That doesn't make me dumb. If I may brag a bit, I took an IQ test in the year 2000 and received the score of 129.

According to certain charts, graphs, ratings and other measurements, that's considered *superior*! On the visual portion of the test I got every question correct. It was noted on the test that I was a "visual genius."

At the time I worked with a guy named Dave who was 45 but looked 35 – one of his many outstanding traits. Dave made it very clear when I arrived on the job that I would not be tolerated, and under no circumstances would I be taking his job. This manifesto was not said in words, per se, but in undermining little digs that came in dripping, snide remarks. Some of them about my intelligence, some about my skills, but mostly about my lot in life. For some reason Dave thought my life-long goal was to be the right-hand man of our boss, who believed a cellophane packet of those square, neon-orange peanut butter crackers was a good bonus.

Because Dave had a superiority complex, he let it be known that he'd recently gotten an IQ test and it was stellar 119. At the time I didn't know if that was good or bad, so I nodded and said "Nice." Mainly because he was beaming with pride over it. He replied "thanks" and asked me what IQ was. You know… normal work conversation stuff. Of course, I didn't know, but that prompted me and another work mate to have ours done.

A few days later I went with my workmate Woytek, a chain-smoking Pole with half a stomach, to have our IQ tests done at the infamous Flatiron Building -- that beige wedge that splits 5th Avenue and Broadway at 23rd street in Manhattan -- about five blocks from our office. The test was administered by a nervous guy who looked like Albert Einstein if Albert was accidentally transported through time and space with a rockabilly musician and they merged. He wore a tweed jacket with leather pants, white hair slicked back and giant, round, steel-framed glasses. Surprisingly, the test was administered on computer, and Albert said very little during the test. At once point Woytek asked if he could have a smoke break and when he was denied, he left anyway.

Afterwards, our tests were printed and I received a 129 and Woytek an incomplete. I was reluctant to tell Dave the result, but Woytek was more than happy to divulge the information. It went down like a bitter pill. Dave pushed a complimentary "very nice" through the mouth slot in his frozen face, but it came off like someone getting the world's worst Christmas gift. "I... love... it."

Bragging about your looks or intelligence is an ugly trait in a person. It's reprehensible and repellant. I don't normally do it. Physicist Stephen Hawking said people who brag about their IQ score are losers. That may be true, but he wasn't a blonde. He didn't have to defend himself. I do! Especially when you're as handsome as I am.

Stephen Hawking never knew his IQ score because he never took an IQ test. He didn't have to. He was solving the mysteries of the universe while most of his contemporaries were scratching their asses. Hawking also never had time to take an IQ test because he was too busy banging chicks. A man who was crumpled into a wheelchair like a wet ragdoll got more action than any of us. He had the voice of a Fisher Price *Speak & Spell*, yet woman fell to their knees to be with him. Maybe they were all Sapiosexuals – people sexually attracted to intelligence. Stephen was crazy famous, wrote bestselling books and had multiple films made about him. I don't have any of that. I have my 129 IQ score to carry around like a badge of honor and I'll wear it with pride.

Blondes are not dumb. No more dumb than any other group. Where did this ideal come from? I'm not a doctor or physician, but hair doesn't grow out of your brain. Anyone who thinks hair color could determine one's brain functionality is a moron.

I suppose the dumb blonde has gotten by on their looks, which caused the brainpower to diminish based on usage. If you're getting by on a pretty face and great body, why use the brain? Sort of like a professional arm wrestler... their right arm is the size of a gorilla leg, and the left as wispy as a broken arm released from a plaster cast. If you don't use one thing as much as the other thing, it atrophies. Looks tend to fade and if you don't use the brain, it can be too late. The proverb *you can't teach an old dog new tricks* applies to human brains as well. Educating a brain early and often is the key to intelligence longevity. If the face and ass slump to match your neglected brain, you could be washed up by 50.

Not only are we blondes supposedly dumb, but we're also having way more fun than everyone else. How hair color can generate fun is not clear either. Perhaps it's color theory. Throw someone in a room with black walls and an hour later, their spirits bottom out like a caged animal. Toss the same person in a pink room and they could go giddy with laughter. Perhaps the same can be said with a blonde-haired companion. Split from your raven-haired buddy and tag along with a sun-glistened blonde and the fun-factor could potentially double. The neon-yellow autumn maple tree packed between a set of muddy green pines definitely gets noticed. But how it equates to fun has yet to be calculated in a laboratory... a lab run by brunettes, of course.

Researchers have studied the effects of blonde hair and have found that blondes are more confident and can make further strides in society. The blonde can be more privileged but also exhibit more aggressive behavior. I'm not sure what methods these researchers used in this research, but I'm not buying it. Were they in a laboratory with bubbling beakers and large chalkboards filled with complicated math equations? What was in those beakers? Champagne? This sounds like unreliable human zoo analysis. Blondes sound like the worst kind of person... dumb, aggressive and oblivious to their privilege. I know lots of blonde sticks-in-the-mud.

There might be a blonde backlash. Back in the 1990s, there was a rock group named 4 Non Blondes. What's up.... with that? That's obviously a name designed to show there's no blondes involved. I don't know if the name is a warning or a welcoming. Maybe the rock group Blondie has an opinion on that.

Where did the notion of the dumb blonde come from?

In popular culture, the first dumb blonde can be traced to a French prostitute, or "courtesan" of the upper French nobility named Catherine-Rosalie Gerard Duthé or simply Rosalie Duthé. After leaving a convent... shocking, I know... she became a frequent companion of French kings and princes. She was often the subject of nude or partially nude paintings, which still exist in many museums and collections around the world. Rosalie was said to have the habit of taking a long pause to think before speaking, a habit I wish more people on the planet would practice. These pauses gave her a reputation of being not only a little stupid, but an outright dummy. Eventually she was the subject of an uproarious comedy play titled *Les Curiosités de la Foire*, an on-going hit in 1775 that had "France laughing for weeks." This is also a country that thought Jerry Lewis was a comedic genius, so take this information with a grain of salt. I'm not sure what Jerry Lewis' IQ was. I don't believe comedic genius is measured through a test. It's subjective. A matter of taste. Like cilantro... it's either deliciously refreshing or tastes like soap. *The Nutty Professor* is a funny film but it's not the *Citizen Kane* of comedy.

Regardless, Rosalie Duthé and *Les Curiosités de la Foire* launched, and perpetuated the dumb blonde stereotype. It also perpetuated the blonde as promiscuous dim vixen -- willing to strip down and spread eagle the moment the opportunity should arise. Anyone not smart enough to speak in continuous sentences without break can surely be manipulated into a bedroom romp.

Stumble 150 years forward and Hollywood perpetuates the dumb blonde in a parade of endless movie performances... its crest reaching when Marilyn Monroe plays breathy Lorelei Lee in *Gentlemen Prefer Blondes*. It's stuck around ever since.

It's been said that Monroe had an IQ of 168, making her smarter than Albert Einstein. That rumor has been proven unfounded and most likely started by a dumb blonde who thought we'd all believe it. Although no record of Marilyn's IQ is documented, it was widely noted among all who knew her that she was incredibly intelligent. Maybe her IQ was more like around... oh, I don't know... 129.

If you can do the math, blonde jokes may predate most 'conditional' jokes by 100 years or so. The Polish joke came about around World War II when German, Russian and Polish immigrants flooded America and they began, or perhaps maintained, a scathing verbal ethnic assassination against the Poles as a country filled with dolts. It not only grew, it spawned endless jokes and joke books that are here today.

My sister's In-Laws are all Polish, including her husband and they're all doctors. Crazy smart people. IQ's off the charts. My brother in-law Jim went to Johns Hopkins and Harvard Medical School and averaged a 4.0 GPA. 4.0!! If you didn't know, that's really good! I also got a 4.0 at Harvard, but that was on a breathalyzer test. That's an easy test to pass.

I'm not sure what Jim's IQ is, but it's probably high. He and my sister Caroline had two girls; my nieces Emily and Amanda, and both are ridiculously smart. Both radiant blondes... and part Polish. They're crushing dumb stereotypes left and right.

As time has marched on, just about every group of people imaginable have become the punchline of a joke. Every ethnicity, religion and occupation has been in the crosshairs of a laugh. All based on preconceived notions, stereotypes and those darn "kernels of truth." Brain-dead blondes, stupid Polacks, big-titted Italians, thieving black folks, boozing Irish, conniving Jews and of course the cut-throat lawyer are all in the mix.

Feel free to defend the target on your back as needed. This one is about blondes.

A good joke can snap, but so can a punch to the face.

Ethnic, racial and religious jokes are all told in good fun, but sometimes the listener doesn't always get the laugh… especially when they're the target demographic. Back in France again, the cartoonists of newspaper Charlie Hedbo mocking the prophet Mohammed found the rebuttal to the butt of their joke came in the butt handle of a rifle. Two Islamic extremists stormed the newspaper offices and killed 12 people and injured 11. Talk about a poor sense of humor.

You won't likely find a pack of wild blondes kicking asses and taking names in the streets. Blondes don't scare people that much – unless they're wearing red swastika arm bands. A pack mentality can be terrifying, but jokes shouldn't cause World War III. We'll leave that to the humorless world leaders who wouldn't know a joke if it came up and tickled their ribs.

Blonde women in particular have the shit end of the stick in the blonde joke arena. Again going back to courtesan Rosalie, then Marilyn, and all the way up to Reese Witherspoon in *Legally Blonde*. They're easy targets. What are they gonna do? Bomb you? They call them blonde bombshells because they're built for sex, not because they contain gunpowder. They don't have violent streaks of revenge set in their chambers. Or maybe they do. Their revenge comes in a slow, meticulous ways that will rear its ugly head when least expected.

I'm the type of person who will marry someone, draw the person into my web of lies, and ten years later, make it all crumble into the sea… just for sweet revenge. Maybe that's because I'm a Scorpio and not just a blonde. Are astrology jokes a thing? Maybe if my moon was in Mars it would make more sense.

TITS AND ASS

Speaking of blondes, my wife is convinced that I'm attracted to tall, Barbie Doll blondes with big tits. Why? Because she's Brazilian and believes that *all* American men like this look. It's what all the Brazilians think. Apparently it's in our drinking water – impossible to expel from our systems. We're pre-programmed to like this type and I can't convince her otherwise.

I've given her a fairly decent list of past girlfriends to dispel that notion, but she still has her doubts. That list contains three Korean girls, a Colombian, two black girls, and a host of other petite, dark-haired women who lean towards the darker end of the skin-tone spectrum.

Unfortunately, I dated ONE blonde girl right before her and that poisoned the well. That one girl erased years of hard-fought dating history and reset the entire timeline.

I'm pretty sure Rita and her fellow Brazilians aren't alone in this summation of United States fetishes. We Americans have this scarlet letter and it's hard to shake. Except the scarlet letter was an A and we're stamped with a Double D. I believe we can trace this back to Hollywood's olden days. A bunch of fat, balding Hollywood execs fell hard for the blonde bombshell type and promoted the hell out of their wishful lust by cramming them into every movie they could.

Some of them weren't even blondes. I know none of them are REAL platinum blondes, but at least some of them start on that side of the fair-haired spectrum. A bottle of peroxide can do wonders, even if the eyebrows are perched atop the eyes like two jarring, gothic crows.

It eventually peaked and continued to ride with Marilyn Monroe, the smoky-eyed honey who walked around like "Jello on springs." She had curves for day, tits like torpedoes, and every word that hushed from her lips, came from the hips and was translated into "take me to bed" regardless of what she said. So the Barbie blonde has become the symbol of all our American lust. Marilyn was in a movie called *Gentlemen Prefer Blondes* for Chissakes!

This idea that all men have the same taste is preposterous of course. That's why when you go to Baskin Robbins ice cream shop, they have 31 flavors and not one, and the pork store will have at least 15 varieties of schnitzengruben. People have different desires. Diner menus are packed with foods I can't image they ever cook, but there's choices, and clothing racks have rows upon rows of endless sizes and colors.

I like petite, dark-haired women. Round butts and little breasts. While most of the men were drooling over Jessica Rabbit on stage, I was searching the room for Betty Boop. She's much hotter and as far as hair and skin tone goes, you don't get much darker than black and white.

Trying and convince a woman with small breasts that you're attracted to small breasts is like trying to get out of jail while you're still holding a smoking gun. It will take more than words to sway that jury. You must produce evidence. You must convince completely... like a cut-throat litigator in a do or die performance. Maybe pull old photos or have old girlfriends lined up and ready to stand trial. To uproot the "American men like big tits" philosophy, which is buried way, WAY down into the dirt, you must dig oh so very, very deep. So deep, even the women can't dig it up.

Many women think they must point out that their breasts are small and joke about it, like a mandatory body check. That's something that's been ingrained in the culture for far too long.

"I know we've taught you that our 'eyes are up here,' but look down here and see if my breasts work for you."

Naked dating seems like an ideal introduction. Maybe go right into sex and talk about interests afterwards.

"You collect clown lamps? Me too!"

That way we can measure everything up at the start. Nothing could be worse than dating someone for months then realize they don't have the penis size you've been hoping for. Sexiness comes from the soul... from confidence, but that doesn't always match up with the body we're given. A woman I was really attracted to once told me that she liked men "with muscles!" really emphasizing the word muscles. I looked down and noted that I indeed had muscles... I wouldn't have gotten very far without them, but they weren't the size that she needed to satisfy her needs.

Telling a woman or a man that they have the goods to satisfy is a tough pill for them to swallow. They've been pre-programmed to believe in Hollywood or magazine ideals and we all fall short… in looks and in height. That's why the Dad Bod suddenly got so hot. A few women (or men) admitted that a guy in fairly decent shape with a nice soft coating of chubby on him was just fine by them.

Many people I know are married to people from different parts of the world. That's what happens when you invent airplanes. People get around. They have a chance to see someone beside the three or four people on the street they live on. The guy who fell for the Polynesian girl he saw in the movie can actually go there and see if he can get one himself, and the woman who wanted someone Tall, Dark and Handsome has the choice to visit multiple exotic countries where the borders are packed with men who fit the description.

They say opposites attract. Paula Abdul sang about it in the 1980s while dancing with a cartoon cat. What can I say? I like Betty Boop, some people like Jessica Rabbit and Paula likes MC Skat Kat. Bust a move out of your neighborhood and you may find yourself cutting a rug with someone that might turn your conservative parents pale… regardless of your parent's skin tone.

My buddy Stephen's wife May from Singapore is Chinese. My cousin Jeff is married to a woman from Iran, and my Greek friend Joanna is married to a blonde guy from Ireland.

Speaking of Greek, I personally relate to the movie *My Big Fat Greek Wedding*. It's a good movie. For me it works on so many levels. Mainly because I relate not to Toula, the woman in the film, but to the man – Ian. He was looking for something different, someone unique. He can't quite put his finger on it… and I've been there.

I've had a few groups of people try and set me up with a woman. "I think you guys are perfect for each other" they say, then I get there and I'm like, "NOPE, not even close!" Then I realize "these people don't know me at all!" They haven't seen my Google search history or who my eyes wander to in the coffee shop.

Obviously it's about more than looks, but we're looking for the *total* package, not half the package. Do I like intelligent, funny, down-to-earth women who can shotgun a beer? Of course! But there's another aspect to it. We don't always talk about the whole package to other people. I haven't really told my friends what kind of women I like, although, some of them figured it out on their own. But some people didn't get the memo and it can go terribly wrong.

Friend: "You have to meet my friend Kati!"
My mouth: "Ok. Great."
My brain: Does she look like Penelope Cruz?
Friend: "Super cute. Loves movies and comic books!"
My mouth: "Just my type."
My brain: Please say she looks like Penelope Cruz!
Friend: "I think you'd get along perfectly."
My mouth: "What does she look like?"
Friend: "Kinda like Helen Hunt with curly hair."
My brain: Dammit!

In some cases we should just come right out and tell everyone what kind of people we're attracted to.

"Hi, I'm A.J. and I like Italian, Hispanic, and Pacific

Asian women with olive skin and dark eyes."

"That's great A.J., but this is the annual shareholders meeting."

Sometimes these things can be misinterpreted as a fetish. It's a fine line. If you're doggedly determined to find a Japanese Geisha girl out of every Asian woman you meet, you might have a fetish. But liking Asian women can't be shit-on either. Sometimes we demand inclusiveness and unity, then call it out negatively when acted upon. Which do we prefer? Men who love Asian women, or men who hate them? If it's something that is positive and healthy, then we can choose love every time.

That's why I don't understand racist ideals. Have these people never watched a Miss Universe pageant? Like... specifically the swimsuit portion? I can't imagine these knuckleheads could get through an entire show and not want to bang almost all of them. Separate these guys into interrogation rooms and feed them pictures of scantily clad international models and they'll crack like a 14-year-old boy under hot lights.

Have these people not seen Naomi Campbell in a tiny bikini? Did they not see Halle Berry emerge from the ocean in the James Bond movie *Die Another Day*? What about Selma Hayek dance on stage in *From Dusk Till Dawn*? Who are they trying to fool? Of course they did!

Beauty standards have changed over time. Look at the pre-bombshell movie vixens of the 1920s. All of them assless ghosts... bodies no more shapely than the blanket you tossed over the couch and use on chilly nights... squiggly hair plastered to their heads like ramen noodles. Now the starlets come in all shapes and size. Dark skin, light skin… thin lips, fat lips. Tall, short, skinny and wide. It's a beautiful thing.

A few years ago, my father asked me if I ever heard the song *Baby Got Back* by Sir Mix-A-Lot.

"Heard it? It's practically my anthem." I admitted.

He was satisfied with this answer and began singing the song, which was both awesome and funny because he instantly mangled the lyrics.

Sir Mix-A-Lot and I, both like big butts. It's a matter of personal taste. Some don't like big butts. They like small butts, or small breasts… or big ones. They like tall and small and somewhere in the middle.

There's a flavor for everyone. That… you can't deny.

GODZILLA VS. PARANOID MAN

I'm lying on the couch, lost in thought. My son is crunching on a fortune cookie, which is odd because we didn't have Chinese food for dinner. Whatever. He reads his fortune and it says something about things turning around in a happy way. I'm sure the cookie stated it more eloquently, but that was the gist of it. He's hoping the statement indicates school being cancelled tomorrow because there's snow in the forecast. He's carefully monitoring the situation not only on his phone, but mine as well. We have two different sets of weather apps, both with radars and moisture detectors and they can tell us down to the second when a flake may drop.

I went outside and saw something falling from the sky and it looked similar to plain old rain, but, his fortune and the little wishes in his heart have told him it will be a blizzard. He just had nine days off for winter break and returned to school for one lousy day, yet he's already desperate for school to be cancelled. Not only that, there hasn't been one snow day this year... a tragedy to all children who long for piles of snow to plow through.

"What did your fortune say again?" I ask.

He reads aloud: "Be prepared for a sudden, needed and happy change in plans."

As he's crunching on his admitted second fortune cookie, he starts talking about Godzilla. I'm way off in another world because I'm so far in debt, my gym just cancelled my membership because my credit card is maxed out. I missed two car payments and I'm on the brink of having either a nervous breakdown, or reverting to some old habits, some of which include heavy drinking and a steady diet of staring at the wall and wondering how it all went so terribly wrong. My freelance work dried up, I had a bad month at work, and my paycheck-to-paycheck life came crashing down like a house of glass.

Still, we have food in the house... fortune cookies and I believe some green bananas, but otherwise, I don't think we'll starve. Unless the blizzard comes and they shut off the gas. Then we may freeze. But we have blankets and each other. Unless our bodies stop producing heat from lack of food. Then it really starts going downhill. I mean, it *is* going downhill. Fast. But there's some things we can do to prevent the bleeding. I could sell blood or start doing OnlyFans, but no one wants to see me naked spanking my monkey on camera. I do go to the gym so the body isn't bad. But, the membership was canceled so perhaps my gut may jut sooner than later. Of course, there's limited food, so I may have washboard abs in no time.

Max is hoping his "sudden and needed" change comes

in the form of a snow day and I hope it comes in the form of about $10,000.

"Remember when I told you about all those Godzilla movies they didn't make? Like Godzilla vs. Frankenstein and Godzilla vs. Batman?" Max says.

"Yes." I say. "They didn't sound any more ridiculous than the ones they've already made."

And that's true. They've made a bunch and as the years went on, they got more and more absurd. Besides fighting King Kong, he's battled: a giant moth; Mechagodzilla, which is a giant robot version of himself; an armadillo thing; aliens; the Japanese Army and of course, Raymond Burr. So in the scheme of things, Batman or Godzilla's own ghost don't seem that far-fetched as a lineup of potential foes.

Also like me, Godzilla has a kid – Godzilla Jr. I'm not sure how he falls into the story line. I'm sure Godzilla Jr. is a respectful child, like most Japanese children tend to be, and not like annoying American children who mock their fathers at the dinner table and interrupt them while they're reading.

"Remember Shin Godzilla?" he asks, and of course I don't. I can barely remember an hour ago and he has encyclopedic knowledge of the Godzilla canon.

"Is that like Godzilla's leg?" I ask.

He laughs because, you won't believe this, it's not his shin, but some super pumped-up version of Godzilla that glows, or shoots lasers or crackles with molten lava or something. I lose track because I'm thinking of my finances and Max is showing me multiple images on his phone of various Godzillas shooting various colors out of them.

"There's even Crystal Godzilla." He says laughing.

I imagine a diamond-like Godzilla with a billion cut-sharp angles. He shows me a picture of Crystal Godzilla and it's no more sophisticated than a Godzilla toy left in some rocks and 3 large, pointy quartz chunks grew out of him. The kind of quartz rocks you may find at a gem show, or tied around the neck of a girl whose smoking clove cigarettes and wearing clothing made of hemp. It's not an impressive version of the famous beast.

Crunching on his third fortune cookie, Max smacks his lips and reads off the new fortune:

"Don't worry; prosperity will knock on your door soon."

It can't come soon enough. Even though I'm enjoying my 14th or 15th Godzilla history review, I've grown increasingly concerned about my car getting repossessed by a tough-guy stooge in the middle of the night while I sleep. It's probably the same guy who goes around stealing catalytic converters, but he needs a legitimate thieving job and car repossession is legal, I believe. But, I need money because I need the car to do things like... well... everything. Errands and stuff.

Although the gym membership is canceled, my new workout routine involves jumping up from the couch at the sound of every passing car – waiting for the repossession guy to get out and steal the Jeep. My neighbor Bill had a landscape artist over and when he pulled up in his unmarked pickup truck, I assumed it was a repo man in disguise. Bill is a great neighbor and we love each other, so I don't think he'd sell us out like that, but you never know. He and the guy were pointing at his lawn and the occasional bush, but it could have been a set up. They pointed at bushes, but it's possible they were talking about our parking schedule and when we went to bed at night. It's a "fake left, go right" type of thing. Like ventriloquists. Throwing their voices and that type of trickery. My wife decided to make the ultimate sacrifice. Hours before this stimulating Godzilla recap, while working on my computer, Rita came into my office and plopped her diamond ring into my hand.

"See what you can get for this. But don't take nothing!" she insists.

"I don't want to sell it."

"It's ok. It's just a material thing."

We talked about the ring as a safety net in the past, but I don't want to sell it. It was just a thought, but now we may have to go there. I bridge the subject of her getting a job, and she wants to, but she doesn't know what to do, and she's beset with anxiety – an affliction I'm more than familiar with. She doesn't want to baby sit, or work with food… or work on Saturday or Sunday, and whittles the field down… continuously narrowing the gauge that eventually yields about 3 jobs in the tri-state area. Not to mention she doesn't have a car and our son is in school, so our extra income hopes have fallen on the notion of someone physically coming to the front door and handing her cash, which seems unlikely. Prosperity, although excellent for fortune cookie material, rarely actually knocks on the door. They say you make your own luck and it's true, but that requires a heavy dose of trial and error, as well as getting out and doing stuff. Luck is a word people magically replace with good fortune when you've been grinding behind the scenes like a slave.

Max attempts to put another fortune cookie in his mouth, but it hits the floor. He scoops it up and crunches it.

"Three second rule." He says.

"I thought it was five seconds."

"They've done studies recently where scientists tested out how long a piece of food needs to be on the ground before the germs can get on it. It used to be five seconds on the ground, but now they say it's three."

"Those germs are very fast."

"Yeah."

I have a feeling these scientists are the same guys that are tracking Godzilla. They monitor him under the ocean floor. They wonder how he came to be, this massive, destructive creature. Was he a titan of lost times? A beastly dinosaur that roamed the earth, long before mankind crawled from the mud? Or is he the product of mankind's terrible and careless decisions? Like exploding nuclear devices that contaminated the water and gave birth to this massive misunderstood monster. Or perhaps, in our desire to explore every crevice of the planet, we dug too far and uncovered a sleeping giant.

In one of the films I watched with Max (I think it had aliens, Mechagodzilla, and a red aquatic dinosaur) the main scientist was a mad one. Dr. Shinzo Mafune was raving about how the government had thrown him out of the scientific community for suggesting that there were giant dinosaur-like creatures living under the sea. That in itself isn't so crazy, but he said he could control them with his mind, which is crazy. But it's a Godzilla movie made in the 1970s when people were doing massive amounts of drugs, so not so crazy. But Dr. Mafune turned his daughter into a cyborg… so, crazy again. The aliens recruited the doctor to help them take over the world by controlling this giant red dinosaur and Dr. Mafune wanted revenge, so he jumped on board the plan. This is a perfect example of how unreliable scientists can be when it comes to things like how long cookies can be on the ground before germs invade the sugary treats. Scientists could all be stark, raving mad. Every one of them.

Max crunches a cookie in his mouth. It may have been his fourth cookie. I'm not sure why we have so many fortune cookies in the house. We do get Chinese food a lot, and they tend to toss in giant handfuls of fortune cookies in the bag, but, I thought we threw them out. They also give us this big bag of friend noodles, which are incredibly addictive, and I crunch those until Rita rips them out of my hand and tosses them in the trash.

With the ring in my hand, I went to the jewelry store where I originally purchased the ring for our 10th wedding anniversary. They buzzed me in after examining me through the glass door and determined I was not a criminal or a meth head. The interior glistened like an ice cave. They greeted me warmly. I showed them the ring and slung a story that my wife and I were interested in selling it. We were "liquidating our assets" so we could put a down-payment on a house. I also had some paperwork they originally provided when I purchased the ring. Diamond GIA gradings and other worthless papers. I say worthless because I'm pretty sure polished rocks become even more worthless when you walk out the door than automobile when you drive them off the lot.

"Your wife is so sweet" says Gloria the owner, who

retired a few years ago. But now she's back.

"Yes, she is." I confirm. "But, she wants a house, even though the market is crap."

"Oh, there's nothing out there right now. And the prices are so high."

"I thought you retired." I ask.

Everyone around the room snickers. It was a 'right, retire hahaha' kind of inside joke.

"Oh I did. I just like to work. Plus, the kids... they had some good ideas but they seem to not do things correctly."

She threw her entire family under the bus right then and there. Savage.

"I'm sure they're doing fine." I said in a show of support.

But, it was too late. The young jewelers had huddled down shamefully below eye level. Taping on keyboards and shuffling papers.

We banter about the state of things. The prices, the taxes, the inventory... it's a bitchfest. But, it helps because we know we're all in the same sinking ship together. It's not an isolated thing – I'm not alone. Everyone is dealing with the same shit. Although, these jewelers are standing around cases of diamonds worth millions and when I get home, I'll be standing around stacks of worthless junk.

The jeweler tells me to leave the ring so she can clean it and give it a proper evaluation. I say Okay, but I assume she's going to replace the diamond with a hunk of worthless glass. It's a respectable business that's been in our town for decades, but I assume they're thieves trying to fuck everyone over like shysters. They've given no indication that they're anything but sweet and caring people, but I assume everyone is trying to fuck me over. When I'm down, I'm really down. I get dark and down on myself and everyone I deal with. I need money, but I'm pretending I'm buying a house in the worst housing market in history.

A day later I call and they offer me half what I paid for the diamond, solidifying my stance that the diamond and jewelry market is fixed and that everything purchased is marked up and glorified to the point of fraud. It's worth about as much as a cheap plastic toy you crank out of a gumball machine.

"Just keep it, A.J... Give it to your children when you're older." Gloria says.

"Yeah. That's what I'll do." I say assuredly.

I'm sure my son will love wearing a diamond engagement ring when he's down at the basketball courts, knocking down jump shots.

The next day I retrieved the ring and give it back to my wife. It's a relief because I didn't want to sell it. She smiled so wide, I could sense her joy in having it back. She put it on and continued working on the colorful cupcake puzzle she was puzzling over. I continued to puzzle my brain about where I'm going to find this money I need.

So, I'm on the couch, staring at the wall. The wall has no answers. My son doesn't either. He has colossal amounts of information about Godzilla, but little else. He's 12. Soon to be 13. He's got fortune cookie philosophy and winter wishes. He looks outside for snow.

"Is it snowing?"

"No." I say because I've already got my nose to the window, looking for the repo man.

Now I'm hoping for snow too. A *lot* of snow. Feet of snow. Repo men won't come and take your car in a snowstorm. They would need to clear it off, de-ice it and warm it up... scrape the windows and turn on the defroster. It's ridiculous. No one would do that. Most people hate clearing off their own car. The repo man will most likely wait till Spring, so I have a few weeks till the weather changes. Although, it's been a particularly warm winter.

"I don't like the way they make Godzilla look in the new movies. Like a dinosaur." Max says.

"Yeah. You like the old-school, man in the rubber suit look."

"Yes. I guess so." He admits.

There are no more fortune cookies to crunch. Max has crushed them all – like little Tokyos.

I'm tired. I skipped lunch. I was going to have rice, but we needed it for dinner, so I skipped the whole thing. I drank coconut milk, which no one seems to like in the house – including me. Max wanted it because he thought it would be good, but he took a little sip and then he was out. "I don't like this" he stated. It became my lunch. A big cool glass. I suppose if I was on a desert island and was forced to drink coconut mash, it would keep me alive, but the concoction of water and coconut meat blended into this bastardized milk product is not something I want to live on. Maybe it can be disguised around a giant bowl of sugar bran flakes or crackling rice cereal, but not as a stand-alone refreshment.

It's just as well. I could stand to shed a few pounds.

The less I eat, the less toilet paper I'll need. We only have one roll in the house and for some reason we're transporting it back and forth between the upstairs and downstairs bathrooms. A time-share system. You know times are tough when there's only one roll for multiple butts. Max had a buddy use the upstairs bathroom and call for a roll, but the only one available was the downstairs bathroom roll. It's been making the rounds ever since.

I take Max up to bed and lie down with him. The stars are in the sky. Well, not real stars. The glow-in-the-dark stars we glued to his bedroom ceiling when he was 7. The sound of sizzling is evident. But it's not my brain frying, nor is it food in a pan. It's the sound of frozen rain shushing against the window. His dream of a snowstorm may soon come true. He gets excited and I finally relax. He wants the day off and I want to keep the repo man at bay. A coating of ice may do both.

It doesn't matter if it's a hunched, T-Rex looking beast, or a googly-eyed lizard with excellent posture... the Godzilla-of-life is bearing down on me. My own personal Godzilla. It's smashing buildings, swatting helicopters from the sky and destroying everything in its path. The only way to keep it at bay is to fire money at it – like missiles.

"You think they'll cancel school tomorrow? He asks.

"No." I say trying to burst his bubble.

"Why not?" he asks incredulously.

"The weather app said it was only going to snow a few hours."

"They could be wrong."

"I doubt it."

To steady my nerves, I ask him about Godzilla foes and which are the best.

"There's Destroroyah, he's really good. Most of them are basically dinosaurs. There's Ghidrah, the three-headed monster…"

As he speaks and catalogs his memory as to "who's who" in the monster-verse, my brain tails off and thinks about my own three-headed monster to battle.

A.J. vs. The Cut-Throat Loan Shark
A.J. vs. The Tornado of Swirling Bills
And of course,
A.J. vs. His Old Nemesis – Father Time.

THE STUPID
MACHINE AT WORK

The Stupid Machine, like any semi-conscious beast, has the desire to roam free because they're an animal that inherently thrives without constricting borders. Unfortunately, the Stupid Machine is in a constant state of putting up barriers. They're called walls, fences, gates, barricades and of course, the ultimate death knell, the office cubicle.

The Stupid Machine finds itself inside this manufactured pen like any pig or chicken would find itself on the slaughter farms of the world. They're placed in the cubicle and piled with work until they become so depressed, they're almost despondent. To get them functioning again... lifted from their paralyzing stupor, they're fed fattening, high-calorie foods that are paired with liquids loaded with caffeine. It's the only way to get the miserable bastards through the unconscionable disaster known as the workday.

From 9-5, the Stupid Machine becomes a slave to the artifice of mass consumption. A cog in the industrial wheel that never stops churning, no matter how devastatingly cruel the wheel gets. It doesn't matter if the wheel grinds them all to dust – it moves on, like a mechanical glacier... an unstoppable force that can only be stymied by the complete and total destruction of the human race.

The 9-5 work zone is nothing but a fantastical myth. A fairy tale of nonsense. The workday for the Stupid Machine starts long before they rise at the crack of dawn. Because their nightmares are laced with the terror of their tyrannical bosses and mundane, crippling tasks, they're exhausted to the point of suicide before their bleary eyes are even pried open because they've been working overtime in their dreams. They awaken not only un-rested, but utterly drained of vital essence. Whether they drive, walk or bike to work... or their computer monitors are flashing in their own homes, the workday begins physically the millisecond their tired, aching feet hit the ground. Then, once they've had their brains battered and their dreams dashed into an unconscionable pudding, they return to their home lives, which have zero meaning because they have no time to properly maintain them. Their homes and families are like neglected gardens, dying under the withering sun that is their own hopelessness. The Stupid Machine is connected to the universal tit like a dying humanoid on a dialysis machine. They're unable to disconnect from the phone or internet because their bosses will continue to hound and distract them with work until their heads hit the pillow like they've been mentally pummeled with something resembling the knockout blow of a boxer.

The only real relief the Stupid Machine will get from the driving anguish of their slavish work life is to get devastatingly ill. They can use the few days they're allotted away from the furnaces of industry to regenerate their health. The two or three "sick days" they're gifted can be used for open heart surgery or to cram a life-saving a kidney into their body so they can return immediately to the chains of their indentured servitude and be of some use to their heartless masters who will juice every shred of profit from the pulp of their soul.

When the Stupid Machine is unable to physically escape from the pounding headache of their horrifying reality, they escape mentally by getting blisteringly, cockeyed drunk. They siphon poison into their brains at alarming rates until they not only become a different person, they forget their identity completely. They scream their pent-up frustrations in a howling cry, powered by toxic alcohol and high-powered drugs. Their inhibitions melt as their caged inner-animal is channeled into an embarrassing performance of brash stupidity, which usually ends with teeth smashing into hard pavement or legs spread so the throbbing hammer of pleasure can give them a fraction of connection to something in the world besides cold, hard plastic and steel. A complete memory wipe into blackness, a destruction of the temporal lobe is preferable to any memory of who they are and where they are enslaved each and every dire day.

The payment for this recklessness will be paid in full in a few short hours when they're again forced into the cubicle cell of doom, their skulls splitting in pain like they've been axed like logs and forced to work under the harsh, buzzy fluorescent blue lights of their worst nightmare. The jarring environment is the complete opposite of any warm and cozy bar where they were chanting sing-a-longs with strangers only mere seconds ago. The Stupid Machine spends the entire day, which feels like an eternity, functioning like a zombie until they can go to their beds and recover from their noxious decisions. Of course, the best way to avoid any nagging hangover is to continue guzzling booze and snort medicine uninterrupted until their knee-deep in a dilemma. Perhaps if they're lucky, rehab can give them their desired respite from the daily grind of their crippling work life.

In their desire to free up their time so they can enjoy one second of their private life, the Stupid Machine has actually made their lives more complicated by introducing innovation and progress. Mainly, they've created machines to replace themselves – their advancements so clever and futuristic they find themselves becoming obsolete. Now, the Stupid Machine will be forced to create new jobs to become relevant again. Robot repairperson, computer technician, AI fighter and lubricant hawker. Before long, everyone will be dictating full instructions to these cyborgs and talking to these artificially intelligent robots like they're another human sitting right beside them. Except the response will be ice cold... the voice of an AI computer regurgitating words that have been stolen from a billion conversations which have been spoken and recorded through time.

Every Stupid Machine has a co-worker or two who dreams of killing them for their incompetence, yet will never follow through with the plan because a jail cell is worse than a cubicle. The AI robot has no conscious to stop themselves from executing a prime directive of murder. One day any Stupid Machine could be finishing their lunch, which constitutes nothing more than a pile refined fat and processed sugar, and the next thing they know, the Stupid Machine is lying in a pool of their own blood that is conspicuously mixing with high-viscosity motor oil. The only fingerprint to glean from the crime scene is that of a rubber nub on the finger of a metal clamp… a clamp that is used to fit a microchip into a computer, or twist a lug nut into an automatic weapon.

Even though the Stupid Machine has done everything in its meager power to ease its plight in life, it is still inexplicably working itself to death. While the robot is breathing down its neck to take its place in the world, the confused human beast is struggling to manufacture and operate basic machinery like copy machines, printers and even the wasteful pod coffee maker. When the copy machine isn't replicating their misery in multiples, it's malfunctioning by crunching paper through its sensitive lights and gears. The printer, a machine that presents tangible proof of the Stupid Machine's ceaseless torment, is worth nothing more than a few dollars, but like any fuel-based gadget, runs on ink which costs more than a worker's annual salary. And the caffeine dispensing coffee maker, when not honking and blinking from neglect, brings the only joy the Stupid Machine can find in an endless landscape of defeat. The Coffee machine and its general surroundings is an oasis to find three minutes of quiet time to refuel their dying energy before returning to the blender of mania, which is known as the perpetual workday of madness. Perhaps these machines are constructed with obsolesce in mind, programmed to malfunction upon the simplest of commands – driving their users to such dissatisfaction, they essentially become lobotomized from rage until the only proper office function the Stupid Machine can replicate is the pounding of a stapler.

It's also feasible the Stupid Machine doesn't understand the mechanical simplicity of these office machines because they're more interested in building the perfect beast to replace themselves so they can lighten their heavy work load. Like Frankenstein, they hope to create beautiful monsters to help them, but in actuality, the constructed beasts will stop nothing short of choking them till their heads bloat into purple balloons and pop-off their necks like champagne corks.

Essentially a high-functioning ape, the Stupid Machine claims the highest place on the food chain, yet is deadset on making itself extinct with it's terrible decisions. It's been said that certain factions of monkeys and apes have reached "The Stone Age" in their development. We assume it's because they've been watching the Stupid Machine from afar. Pretty soon they'll be using tools and equipment with the grace of a human. Before long, they'll replace low-level workers until each man is replaced with an ape. I'm sure the march of progress will not skip a beat. The film series *The Planet of the Apes* will no longer be a science fiction fantasy but a living, breathing documentary. Regardless of their status in the working class hierarchy, every Stupid Machine from the ditch digger, all the way up to the genius-level CEO will be swapped out with an ape, who no more than a few years ago, did nothing but eat and toss their own shit around like senseless brutes. Like an on-coming army of quadrupedals, these hairy varmints will lift their dragging knuckles off the ground and rise upon two feet where they'll replace the shit in their hands with books and contemplate the benefit of the bomb.

The ape will either use our monetary system or develop their own series of trade. Perhaps working in lock-step with the rising AI machines, they can collaborate on how best to avoid the mistakes of the Stupid Machine, having literal centuries of history to glean the information and study as to why the Stupid Machine continuously shot itself in the foot.

Once every man, woman and child is out of work and living in the woods, they'll have plenty of time to contemplate how they got there. They'll finally have the desired free time they've been craving their entire working life, but no money to pay for their endless health issues created by working themselves into a puddle of problems inside the endless rows of cubicles. They'll become fertilizer faster than they'll procreate and pretty soon the AI Machines will work for each other, creating products for no one but the quickly developing ape.

Ironically, this system of total collapse will be the only thing to save the Stupid Machine from a life of terrible ugliness. Because of their ability to lose control of their lives and turn it over to the machines and the apes, they'll accidentally discover the freedom they've long been striving for. The freedom to create art using mud and crushed rocks... to create music with tree sticks and hollowed stumps... and develop a new religion whose foundation is nothing more than what the sun has shone upon them, and what the wind whistles in their naked ears. They'll enjoy air and the clear blue sky for the first time in generations as they've finally escaped the brutality of the darkened cubical, a place that is known to collect and crush dreams at the most alarming of rates. The veil of depression will be lifted and a new life gifted upon them like the dawning of a new age.

Truly, the only way for the Stupid Machine to emancipate itself from the shackles of slavery that was created by the machinations of their own greed and vanity, is for the world to collapse around them in cataclysmic anarchy. Only then, after everything has completely fallen apart and burned into embers in heaping piles of death can the beauty and simplicity of life be rediscovered under a fresh and clear-eyed perspective of hope. Like a phoenix rising from the smoking ashes of their past mistakes, the Stupid Machine can step into a new life where the only worry they'll have is how to redirect the fresh stream waters into their mouths, how to collect the growing fruit they've plucked from the blossoming trees, and how they're going to construct the weapons of mass destruction to reclaim their former lives from the intelligent machines and dirty, filthy apes.

SUMMER
DAZE

I was taking the final exam for Mr. Salzman's 9th grade algebra class when everything on the page abruptly flipped to something resembling Chinese – except with numbers. Nothing on the page made sense, so I freaked out, shot up from my chair, mumbled "fuck this," walked to Mr. Salzman and left a crumpled paper ball on his desk. Mr. Salzman looked at me confused as I headed towards the door. I heard Meredith shout "A.J.!" like a person would shout to a jumper about to leap in front of a train. She knew what the results would be if I walked out the door… summer school. At that point it was too late. Meredith's desperate words hung in the air like musket smoke as I walked out the door and into the hall.

That moment was actually the biggest kerfuffle I ever made in school. Although a jokester, I was a fairly respectable person in class. But, that test inexplicably drove me over the edge. I don't know where I went after that. It was all a blur. The next memory I have is going to summer school, where

I had... Mr. Salzman... or as we affectionately called him, Cerebal Salzy. My buddy Bob bestowed that moniker during a flying fit of rage where his flapping lips spouted waves of spit on us – like Daffy Duck. These bouts of rage were usually caused by my inability to focus, while giving wise-ass answers. Usually when a teacher asks for the answer to a math problem, it's followed by numbers. My answers were usually long-winded statements filled with words.

Bob's grades were all 100s so he wasn't going to summer school. He was a good student. He naturally absorbed information. I didn't. Especially math. It bounced off my brain like a well-pumped basketball. Bob tried to help me but it was hopeless. I fell into the hands of Cerebal Salzy once more. This time in the unforgiving heat of a Huntington High School classroom.

Built like a brick pizza oven, the school sits high on a hill without a single tree to block the sun as it crosses the sky for miles, baking each student like a mozzarella stick. At the time, the school didn't have air-conditioning because it was built during a time when men carried blocks of ice up 50 flights of stairs using metal tongs, and an automobile cost a nickel. Because both my parents worked, I had to ride up this hill every morning on my father's bike, a French racing bike with wheels so thin, if you put a needle to them, they could play music. Not only was the school sweltering hot, my Tour-de-Huntington worked an internal heat inside me that sent most people to the hospital.

I asked my parents if I could have a moped or scooter or something to get me around, but they presented me with the fact I would get a car in the "near future" and funds should be diverted to that. Besides, riding a bike uphill in blistering humidity builds character. I claimed my character was built through the humiliation of going to summer school, but that argument fell by the roadside.

There are fewer things more depressing than summer school. While you're locked in a cement room with other dense-minded teenagers, your intelligent friends are swan-diving into pools, sipping on ice-cold beverages glistening with condensation, and talking to other cute, hormone-raging teens on the beach. By the time I got out of class, the day was half over and my friends were knee deep in plans. To have to double back and mix me into the fray would be too much trouble. They were long gone... cruising down the highway, top down, shirts off... uncorking champagne like fireworks.

I'd be forced to eat a tuna sandwich at lunch in an empty house and pray the phone rang.

Cerebal Salzy was an intolerant man, matched only by my intolerance to absorb math. How my grandfather, a mathematician and my father, an architect, managed to have their commutative pedigree grind to a halt in the field of math comprehension by producing a child so terrible at it is beyond anyone's understanding. Mr. Salzman was no doubt reaching retirement age because to teach summer school, a miserable dispatch of lost souls, was to attempt a last cash-grab before retiring to a place where, if he was lucky, he didn't need math nor see any teenagers try and do it.

Salzy was balding and his grey hair shot out to the sides like wings. He tended to clutch it and pull on it to keep from beating us to pulps as I'm sure it was his inherent desire to do so. He barked, frothed at the mouth and tapped on the blackboard so hard, I'm surprised the U.S. Air Force didn't mistake it for Morse Code. I'm not entirely sure, but I believe he wore a red shirt every day, or perhaps that's how I remember him as he was in a state of five-alarm fire rage all Summer long.

I don't remember how long summer school was, maybe five weeks, but I somehow got through. I don't believe I did any actual learning. I don't think it's possible to take what one could learn (or in my case, not learn) in 10 months and pack it into 5 weeks and consider it absorbed into a cranium. That theory holds true because the NEXT year I returned to summer school again. For math.

My 10th grade math teacher, Mrs. Gleicher, was a sweet and kind teacher who did her best to help me absorb math during the course of the year, but her efforts were in vain. Her class was where I created my second biggest kerfuffle in a classroom, except it wasn't a math test meltdown. A guy named Keith, who sat behind me, gifted me a massive jawbreaker candy to suck on, which I proceeded to swallow and choke on. In Mrs. Gleicher's place that day was a substitute teacher, a frail young woman who looked freshly plucked from the depths of a library basement. When I stood and stumbled towards her, clutching my throat to make the universal "I'm choking to death" signal, she looked at me wide-eyed, said, "Oh, dear" then turned to the class and asked casually if anyone knew the Heimlich Maneuver. Her question was met with 25 sets of owl eyes staring back in confusion… almost like she'd asked a math problem or something. The substitute gently took me by the wrist and said, "let me walk you to the nurse." "Nurse?!" I thought, "I'll be dead by then!" I grabbed a chair, threw myself over the back of it and launched the jawbreaker onto the floor.

I know millions of people over the years have complained about algebra and its usefulness in the real world. Some say we should probably teach kids how to do their taxes; but may I heed the call about teaching the Heimlich Maneuver? The only people who knew how to do it that day were me and the chair. Perhaps we need to get those numbers up.

The numbers that did go up during the year were the integers in complex math problems. The numbers that didn't go up? My grades. It was another year of summer school for me.

By this time, I had that car my parents and I had been planning on for the past year. A car we got for free. No funds were diverted to it at all. It was an orange 74 Ford Capri. This baby was a real machine. Like my high school, it also did not have air-conditioning. In fact, the car would overheat so not only did it not have AC, I had to drive with the heater cranked to divert heat from the engine. If you took a ride with me you were guaranteed to exit with sweat pouring down your legs and a beet-red face under a mop of dripping wet hair.

To my dismay, the Capri died two weeks into summer school. The car was free; what did we expect? I've had sandwiches with a longer shelf life than that car. Cruelly, I was back on the Peugot, the French bike the guy at the bike shop convinced my dad to buy... building more fortifying character for me. The tires on the Peugot wouldn't inflate unless we used a fancy attachment on the pump, and the bike had about 35 gears, all of them worthless but a few. One day I slipped and my leg cleaved into the endless rows of gear teeth on the back wheel, causing a gnarly, greasy welt that lasted the entire summer. People would ask me about it for months until the blood in my calf turned green, which repelled people enough to stop asking.

Believe it or not, I had Cerebal Salzy for summer school math again. When he saw me, he was sympathetic. He knew there was a serious disconnect happening and he was attentive and helpful. Still, it didn't stop me from daydreaming. He would talk about X and Y and I saw football schematics in my head. My friends tossed footballs to each other in the ocean surf, while I sat in a classroom with an old man and his pit-stained red shirt.

The smallest of joys I had with Summer school was the downhill ride home. Pretty much from the school to my door was a one-way ticket to paradise. Wind in the hair, cranking the French gears as hard as they could crank until I matched, and even exceeded, a car's speed. While screaming down a sharp hill called Briarwood Drive one day after school, I hit Woodbury road and sailed into town when a car turned into the Chase Bank and I SLAMMED into the hood, flew over the car and onto the parking lot's hot, jagged blacktop. If I had been paying any attention to my algebra lessons, I probably could have determined what angle I flew into the air and at which degree I fell, but I wasn't paying attention so my best hypothesis was that: while in the air I was shaped like a Y and fell on my Pi hole directly onto an X marks the spot.

I scraped and rolled until I heard a guy shout "oh my god!" When I came to my senses, I saw a long-haired guy with an Ozzy Osbourne T-shirt standing over me distraught.

He thought he'd killed me, and he may have if I hadn't taken Jiu Jitsu and knew how to tuck and roll properly. After this guy pulled himself together, He checked to see if I was alright… and I was. He on the other hand, was a wreck. Most likely stoned, and maybe, another moving violation from having his license revoked, he begged to let him drive me home immediately. Probably to avoid police activity. I don't remember what his car was exactly, but it was a big, expensive, dark blue thing and it didn't match his overall appearance, so he either stole it, or it was his father's. I could sympathize. My father wouldn't be happy to see his expensive French bike twisted like a pretzel just as much as his father wouldn't want to see the deep impression of a French bike in the side panel of his expensive car.

After he dropped me off, I had a severe limp and noticed the bike was slightly misaligned. I missed an opportunity to milk the moron for some cash, but I was still in a daze from the accident.

To my great sadness, the bike still worked and I was forced to ride it to school. The one thing the accident did make unusable was the hand pump the bike came with. It bent like boomerang. Not only did the tires require a fancy tire nozzle to inflate, the pump was worthless and when the air pressure went low, I had to basically ride on metal rims, which felt like a baseball pitcher was throwing stones at my ass.

Eventually I got through math and summer school and I never saw Cerebal Salzy again. In fact, I never took math again in high school. It was glorious. From 11th grade on, I never once dealt with a denominator, a quotient, nor had to figure out the percentage of anything other than the tip on a dinner check.

It was a steady diet of English, art, social studies and more art.

Although I saw less 'lesser thans' than ever before, my shock was greater than great when I failed Social Studies and had to go to summer school for the THIRD year in a row. Oh, the humanity!

This go around, we diverted those car fund into an actual functioning vehicle that transported me to school... a rusting, brown Jeep Renegade. We bought it off some sleazy guy we found in the local newspaper's classified ads – the wild west of buy and sell transactions. He assured us the rattling sound it made was just a loose belt and could easily be fixed. Making the Jeep a true original was a pair of bullhorns mounted to the front. I believe it was the main selling point. This Jeep missed its calling by living on Long Island and not in Texas where bulls are a dime a dozen. Of the Jeeps many charms, it had 33" tires and a V8 engine that could blow any car off the line for the first 3 seconds. After that, it began to drift and catch air because it was essentially a tool shed on wheels.

Unfortunately, my friends all had cars too, so not only were they off making plans, they were leaving town and sometimes leaving the state. While I was toiling away in the hot box of school, they were falling in love on rocky shores while waves crashed and the sound of freedom filled the air. To compensate for my loneliness, I jammed a mannequin in the passenger seat of the Jeep to keep me company. I found him... or should I say, I *stole* him during a lunch break one day towards the end of the school year. Maybe if I'd been spending more time in class and less time stealing things, I may have passed. A small clothing store near the bagel shop was going out of business and the mannequins were all waiting outside to be shipped to their new residence. I snatched one and dressed him in a red Hawaiian shirt... fit him like a glove. We basically had the same body but he had a better tan. People in traffic would start conversations with him before realizing he was a dummy.

My 11th grade Social Studies teacher was Mrs. Morrison, a well-known lush. At least, that was the rumor. I couldn't truly know as most of the people in my family exhibited the same wobbly attitude, so she seemed perfectly fine to me. When she wasn't groggily staring out the window, she was barking orders at us. Our last major assignment for the year was a paper about a hot social issue – as this was social studies – to be presented with facts and charts and graphs and things of that nature. Considering I didn't know anything that was happening in the world outside the general area in front of my face, I struggled to find a topic. Every time I marched to her desk with an idea, she barked "Not specific enough!" My friends were knee deep in politics, terrorism and crime. I made my final march to her desk with the topic of airline safety, and was given a "not specific enough, but pretty good!"

With the help of my friend Bob, we created a paper that was right out of the school of Arnold Schwarzenegger films in its scenarios of plane safety, and people's ability to high-jack one based on things Arnold did in the movie *Commando*. Without one fact, chart or graph to support anything I wrote... not even a footnote... my paper crashed and burned and punched me a one-way ticket to summer school. Even though my fellow students seemed to pass the class, I chalked up my failure to Mrs. Morrison's drinking.

If a student was to ever be broken like a wild horse, summer school is the institution to make it happen. Any savage beast with fiery dust spewing from their flared nostrils will undoubtedly be humbled to a kitten under the unforgiving boredom and dread of summer school. Minutes pass like hours… days like millennia. To watch that slow, skinny, red second-hand of the clock rotate around its bland face, is to know the pain and suffering of the shipwrecked man as he scratches yet another line on the cave wall – marking his slow, yet certain demise.

You look around at your scholarly cell mates; all of them idiots and clearly headed for the dust bin of life, and they in turn, look back and think the same thing about you. "How did we all get here?" is the common denominator in thought.

Compounding the misery of this Summer School tri-fecta was my Social Studies teacher, Dr. Snyder. Usually when you have the title of doctor before your name, you can mend broken bones, a broken psyche, or at least resuscitate a horse. I'm not sure what Dr. Snyder was a doctor of, but it wasn't medicine, or psychiatry, or anything that could help cure a human in any way. He was a social studies teacher. His family paid good money for him to spend the better part of three decades in school so he could sit in a schoolroom sauna with me and my fellow morons. Even if he knew quantum physics it'd mean something, but Dr. Snyder was a man resting on a title and his glib, self-satisfaction was off-putting.

Dr. Snyder was a know-it-all and I knew this because I had him as my 10th grade social studies teacher, a class I somehow passed. Dr. Snyder was the living incarnation of Peter Griffin from the show *Family Guy*, except without the stupid charm. Somehow I passed this summer class too. Maybe he was a better teacher than I remember. Couldn't tell you any social events papers I handed in to pass the class. Maybe a detailed synopsis of the Jean Claude Van Damme classic *Bloodsport*. I don't think the requirements to get through Summer school are all that difficult. The ability to nod and fog a mirror is about it. I believe if you show up, they give you a sympathetic pass. You're in summer school... they know you'd rather be a million other places besides school. They're teachers, not monsters.

That was my final year in Summer school. That's because the next summer I was done with school and got a job. You know, the school of hard knocks. So in reality, my last autonomous summer before a depressing rerun of summer school, tedious manual labor, and life's crushing adult responsibilities was the summer before ninth grade. When I was thirteen. Those were glorious times. Math was nothing more than addition and subtraction; social issues consisted of me controlling my awkwardness at parties and gatherings; the only doctor I saw was an allergist who graduated from a school of medicine, and the only school I visited was a movie theater, where I watched Marty McFly travel back in time so he could go to high school with his parents. All of them smart enough to avoid summer school.

IT'S JUST
A FANTASY

"Fantasy Sports cost U.S. companies $435 Million per week in lost productivity."

This is a stat that's thrown around three times a year in some article written by a guy who needs to fill a financial news quota on Marketwatch, CNN Business or on Anne's Reindeer Jerky Farm newsletter. The article miraculously co-incides with fantasy football, baseball and basketball seasons. Hunting season too, probably.

When you read a number like $435 Million, you probably nod and say: "yea, that sounds about right." If the same line read, "Fantasy Sports cost U.S. companies $921 Million per week in lost productivity" or "$287 Million per week in lost productivity" you'd probably say: "yea, that sounds about right." Why? Because we get stats like this from the internet, a place with so much misinformation, stories about our gay orgy-loving President anal probing people with reindeer jerky barely raises an eyebrow. Mainly because it's offered as truth and either accepted as that, or discounted as ridiculous. I mean, where do you think I got the number $435 Million per week? From the internet of course!

But the crux of the issue is this: God forbid we Americans look away from our meaningless jobs for 5 minutes to adjust our fantasy sports lineups and get a moment of joy in our brutal and pointless existence! If our bosses could turn their violent ire towards their family for a second, we can swap our backup quarterback into our fantasy football lineup when our regular QB sprains his thumb. It's the simple things in life that give it meaning.

News articles like these practically write themselves. All the writer has to do is factor in the time spent playing fantasy sports during work hours and equate it to money. It's an easy article to keep in the archives and bust out like a flashlight in a storm. Just plug it into your website when the regular news hyperbole grinds to a halt. Once in a while the cycle will balance out the grim reality with a positive story. Equating lost revenue to fantasy sports is a little bit of both. It's a glimpse into the popularity of fantasy sports, but also a reminder from Big Brother to keep your eyes on your work and do your personal shit on your own damn time.

The mistake in the $435 Million price tag equation is factoring time with money. Obviously time is worth money -- LOTS of money -- but discounting fantasy sports as a time waster is a mistake. Fantasy Sports is not only an exercise in team-building and creative management, it showcases problem-solving while stoking competitive fires.

"U.S. companies spend up to $511 Million per month on company management educational programs and team building seminars."

OK, I completely made that number up... but it's totally plausible, right? I may toss that tidbit on the internet and see what news group bites on it. I hear Anne's Reindeer Jerky Farm is hard-up for content. Still, I'm sure U.S. companies spend ridiculous amounts of money on team building programs when people are self-imposing management skills through fantasy sports every day.

Trust me, I've been involved in some of these team-building seminars and the only thing they build is team whining and blaming skills. I'm sure there are more constructive methods to build camaraderie than with the dreadful sessions I've been a part of. I consider a field trip to a local bar to get shit-faced drunk with co-workers far more enlightening. It makes for great team-building because you need to peel each other off the floor like road workers, drag each other into cabs like soldiers, all while debating the pros and cons of stopping two workmates from dry-humping on the jukebox.

Throughout a fantasy sports season, every owner has made at least one or two roster moves that made them sit back and say: "that was a brilliant." Why wouldn't that apply to job management skills? Fantasy teams are excellent training for applied workplace paradigms. At least that's what I tell myself when half my players are on a bye week and I'm scrambling for replacements while my office building is burning to the ground around me. Most bosses could only *dream* of an online training program that tests management and team-building skills in a safe environment. But, they have it at their disposal. They should REQUIRE their employees to have a fantasy sports team! That's MY fantasy. Sad, isn't it?

The people in your fantasy league who do the worst are the people who put the least amount of time into their fantasy team. That neglect destroys their team. Do they neglect their work life the same way? I don't want these shiftless layabouts on my work crew!

Now, I realize that the opposite can also happen. I've worked really hard on my fantasy team and still made costly lineup boners. What killed my teams more than anything was second-guessing my decisions and going against my gut. That's when I lose. Of course, most people who do fantasy sports or gamble their money "go with their gut" and they're basically living in the gutter. One time I put Kyle Lowery of the Miami Heat into my lineup, but switched him out at the last minute because he was 87 years old. I went against my gut. Kyle went ape-shit and dropped 87 three-pointers in the game and was the second highest scorer. That terrible decision cost me thousands of dollars. Did I mention I don't like Kyle Lowery anymore? Completely irrational on my part, but I don't care. Screw him. Anyway, once you start putting money into fantasy sports, you're gambling.

"NCPG estimates that the risk of gambling addiction grew by 30% in just three years."

With the advent of sports betting apps, our work productivity not only drops, but so do our bank accounts. It's easy to funnel money into an app and toss five or ten bucks on a few Sunday afternoon football games. I do it once in a while myself. It's a guaranteed money loser. The second I hit the submit button, I lose half the players in my lineup to injury, and the wide receiver whose having a pro-bowl season will have one catch for 12 yards and net me 1.4 fantasy points. Then I'll stupidly check the leaderboard of players who are statistically having a great day and it's a spreadsheet of the most random players. Guys you've never heard of before. Usually it's the back-up running back of the running back in my lineup because my guy twisted his ankle 3 minutes into the game and the backup is decimating the other team's defense to the tune of 32 fantasy points. It's enough to make me want to throw my phone across the room, but the phone costs $1,200 and throwing a mini handheld communication computer across the room is dumber than sports betting itself.

Fantasy sports has evolved tremendously over the years. Mostly because of the computer. In the early days, you had to look through newspapers and sporting lines and tally-up the fantasy numbers with a pencil like a bookie from 1927. Green eyeshade visor being optional.

Now, the fantasy sports websites tally the information for you. Fantasy sports apps are so easy to use, you only need one finger. The other fingers can do things like lift Doritos and beer to your face, or send a call to voicemail that's most likely a creditor trying to get a missed payment because you've been funneling money into sports apps.

The Covid Pandemic increased the betting totals by leaps and bounds.

Before the smart phone, gambling happened out in the streets. The racetracks were filled with disheveled hobos who looked as if they'd been jerked off a few thousand times. When they couldn't make it to the track, they went to OTB (Off Track Betting) stores. If you aren't old enough to remember these gems, they were places for those disheveled bums who looked as if they'd been jerked off a thousand times to mingle outside on the sidewalk like heroin addicts looking for a fix. Most OTBs have the charm of your average soup kitchen and the patrons look as if they've been jerked.... well, you get the point.

Now everything is on the computer. There's a slew of sports betting and gambling apps. The Vegas giants have now crept onto your phone because they love to siphon your cash anywhere you want to be. You no longer need to be at the swanky hotels where the jangling slot machines and jittery lights ricochet around to lure you in. The Vegas giants will make you go bankrupt while you're cutting the cake at your child's birthday party, sitting on the couch, or even while you sleep.

Sports betting is pretty much everywhere now. It's so prominent that the NBA and the NFL have set limits into how much their players are allowed to be involved. The answer – not at all. They give player orientations about keeping their nose clean. It's the reason Pete Rose has been banned from baseball and others have been exiled over time.

Fortunately, most players don't spend their money gambling... they spend all their wealth on dumb shit that loses value almost immediately. Like cars made of glass and jewelry cut into custom shapes no one would ever want; guaranteed to be worth nothing more than its weight after being melted into ingots.

Before long we'll be able to gamble on just about everything. Even the Special Olympics, which just seems wrong. Putting mentally, physically and financially challenged people and their families in the vulnerable position of gambling and the sharks who run it seems like a recipe for disaster. Although, most people are mentally, physically and financially challenged, we just don't say it out loud. They're the morons of the world. The downtrodden, uneducated idiots who think gambling is a job and scratch-off tickets are their one-way ticket to paradise.

Perhaps the fantasy/gambling machine can find other things to bet on so there's no innocent people caught in the wake. Like, how many hotdogs someone can jam up their ass, or how far we can launch a disgraced judge into a river.

Fantasy sports are not only a safe place to test the limits of your management skills, but they can also be a place to channel your energy. If they remain monetary-free, they can be an escape from our work and personal life... a place to command a virtual army where you're the general that places the troops based on their strengths.

But, like any prudent and rational person, I gave up fantasy sports years ago. I walked away right in the middle of the football season – and I was the Commissioner! I was the one who started the league! I recruited my family and friends and got everyone hooked. Then I walked away. Went AWOL. Like a soldier with PTSD who escaped and dropped acid instead of dropping bombs.

It was the best decision I ever made.

Sure, fantasy sports are a great escape. That's why it's called 'fantasy.' But it can also drive you into a state of immersive mania. The player injuries, the second-guessing, the bad line-up decisions, and the time wasted staring at the numbers as they slowly tick in. All of it enough to make anyone want to escape into another place of fantasy... like the imagination.

In my imagination, I own the sports teams. A football team. I make everyone play fantasy football and whoever wins the league becomes the new vice-president and the loser, regardless of their current position, becomes the janitor. Imagine how much the employees would be involved in fantasy football. Their job requirement will be to not only play fantasy sports, but to master it for their livelihood!

"53% of employed U.S. adults who quit their job, changed their occupation or field of work at some point last year."

RAIN
DELAY

Ominous, charcoal-gray clouds rolled over the island, marching behind a thin frontline of billowy white clouds like a duvet cover blanketing the earth in night. Then, the rains came in perpetual sheets, which didn't relent for three days.

When heavy rain came, my uncle Paul would have smaller interior paint jobs lying in wait when outside work couldn't be done. This rain delay was no exception. He asked me if I wanted to take the work or a few days off. It had been a long, hot summer, working in the unforgiving sun. Usually days spent baking in the sun were good for drying the alcohol that saturated our bodies, but once in a while, it was necessary to stay indoors and let it marinate.

I chose the days off.

I took cover from the rains and all of life's troubles at a big Sheraton Hotel near the Long Island Expressway. An escape. A little R & R. I checked in with nothing but the clothes on my back and Toni. We went immediately to the bar and drank Manhattans.

Two months earlier, while Pat Fitzmaurice and I were sprawled on someone's deck at the condominium complex we were painting, we finally caught a face-to-face meeting with the striking dog walker we'd been seeing for weeks – a bleached-blonde woman with hair chopped in a bob that partially covered her eyes. Pat and I were staring over the harbor inlet, drinking cold water and acting as if like we owned the place, waiting for our friend and my roommate Paulie to deliver beers via his Boston Whaler.

Toni the dog walker always wore cutoff jean shorts and a white button-down shirt knotted at the waist. Her job was to chase grass-chewing Canadian Geese off people's lawns with her blonde Labrador Retriever, Zero. If there was ever was a white-collar job disguised as a blue-collar job... that was it.

"Hello!" I shouted when she finally approached within earshot.

"Hello!" she rang out, returning a big smile and arcing wave.

Zero yanked her along, determined to maim and kill geese as he thought it was his job. I'd learn later he'd already gotten one and was doggedly determined to get another.

"You haven't seen a guy driving a small boat, have you?" asked Pat. "Blonde guy. Chubby. Fast boat. Driving slowly?"

"No." she said. "Why?"

"We're expecting a fresh shipment of beer." I explained.

"Right!" she said. "Contraband!"

"Exactly." said Pat.

"I'll keep my eye out." she assured us with a giggle.

"Please do!" said Pat.

"We're very thirsty!" I said.

A few days later while making a lunch run, I spotted Toni sitting on the curb in a parking cul-de-sac, patting Zero on the head. I asked her if she wanted an iced tea. She said yes and I returned with an ice tea the size of a five-gallon bucket. While she contemplated the sheer immensity of the Styrofoam cup, I asked her out on a date.

We went for sushi at Bonsai, the go-to sushi place in town. I knew the chef and owner whose name was Hiro. I went to school with his children, but I knew him personally because I bartended at the dive next door, where he'd often come for a late night drink. His appetizer specialty was ka-kiyakamoto – pan fired oysters in butter and egg. I know it sounds like a slimy mess, but they were absolutely amazing. I was never one to believe in the oyster as an aphrodisiac, but the way Hiro prepared them, they sure as hell worked. After we dined in the restaurant's quaint back garden, Toni caught me off guard in the parking lot. She hooked my arm and threw me on top of her, crashing onto the hood of an expensive Mercedes. She grabbed my ass and moaned "make love to me" as a young family scuttled their children away in horror. It was 8:00pm on a summer evening… the sun still shining.

I don't really think her behavior was oyster related. She only had a few and didn't sip one alcoholic beverage the whole night. I suppose you could chalk it up to my raging masculinity, but even that was questionable as I was nothing more than a muscular string bean. Perhaps, I was just her type. After I peeled myself off the Mercedes, we got in my car; a sleek and stylish silver Volvo station wagon with black interior that my parents handed down to me. The "family truckster." Toni was on my lap before I could put the keys in the ignition. Her ass hit the steering wheel and bleeped a short honk, which broke her into a fit of giggling. Her hands cupping my face as her hair fell across my forehead.

I hit the gas and zoomed to Heckscher Park and parked – a small park in town with a pond, walking paths and bridges. We split the dusk towards the center of the pond and snuck quietly across a bridge to an island with a bench made of cemented stones and wooden planks.

The lights of town shimmered off the water as the sun went down over the horizon. She looked at me nervously and climbed on my lap… her mouth agape with excitement. I yanked off her shorts, released myself and she slid down over me. The thrill of being exposed on the island was driving us mad with lust – moaning in whispers.

Toni had confessed to me that she wanted to sneak into my house one morning while I slept, slide into my bed, give me a blow job, and leave without saying a word. That dream, I told her, was thoroughly achievable… mainly because Paulie and I never locked our front door. It wasn't unusual to come home to find our friends sitting on our couch, watching TV and drinking our beer.

I never knew when Toni would show up. I wouldn't see her for days, then the door to my bedroom would squeak open. I'd crack my eye open and see the outline of her body in the door frame. She'd get low, her blonde hair disappearing under the covers while I was still in half a dream – her warm body pressed against my legs. She'd bring me to rapture and slide out ... looking at me with a smile and leave, true to her word, without a word.

The two of us got to screwing in all sorts of fun and exciting environments. At the movies, in the car, under the car, in darkened corners, in my bed, and occasionally in her bed. One evening while strolling through an alley, we noticed the side door of an abandoned building was ajar. We dashed up to the top floor where the dilapidated place was a few pipes short of crack house. We screwed in front of the windows overlooking town, then ransacked the place for stuff. Besides old clothes and furniture, there were multiple boxes filled with Wayne/Jayne County *Rock 'N Roll Cleopatra* CDs. I still have a copy in a box somewhere.

The two of us were drinking at the Sheraton bar, knocking back Manhattans and the occasional Rob Roy, which is essentially the same drink; Scotch or Whiskey with Sweet Vermouth and bitters. The giant, race-track oval bar was showcased like an arena in the middle of a swank, open area, surrounded by boxy grey chairs in small clusters around tables, each beset with an incandescent lamp. The place was virtually empty except the two of us, the bartender, a barback, and an elderly couple wedged into a set of boxy chairs near the entrance.

After a few cocktails had drained through me, I went to use the men's room. I crossed the large lounge and down a corridor, around a large rotunda until I reached the men's room door. Having finished, I was making my way back around the

long-curved wall when Toni rushed me like a woman pos-
sessed, snatched my hand and yanked me to the men's room.
We crashed through the door and into the first stall – kissing
passionately. She threw herself against the wall and propped
her foot up on the toilet tank. I yanked up her skirt – no pant-
ies. I dropped my pants and spiked her. She wailed so loud I
thought we'd wake the penthouse. She pulled me tight and
writhed in passion – fucking like animals. I listened to her
moans in one ear and for the inevitable police raid at the bathroom door with the other.

"Tell me when you're gonna cum," she pleaded, "do
it in my mouth."

"Okay." I huffed.

I pumped a few more times and she screamed.

"I gonna cum!" I shouted.

I pulled out, but I couldn't make it to her mouth and
orgasmed on her leg.

"Sorry." I told her.

"It's okay. Don't worry. That was amazing."

She had a bar napkin in hand and used it to clean herself. She fixed my hair and I adjusted her skirt.

"Go!" she told me and pushed me out of the stall.

I composed myself as best I could and exited the
men's room. The door swung open seconds later and Toni
rushed me again, this time more gently. She leaned her head
on my shoulder and scooped her hand around my elbow.

We stumbled back to the bar, dizzy and smiling.

"Let's go up to the room." I said.

"Sure."

I sank the last of my drink, threw some money on the

bar and thanked the bartender.

"No problem." He said smirking.

The bartender was a smarmy little prick. Black, slicked-back hair and a pencil-thin moustache. Someone right out of a 1920s crime thriller. He flashed a big smile at me – like he knew a secret I didn't know.

I headed towards the elevators and when I noticed Toni wasn't with me, I turned back around. She was still at the bar, knees up on the stool and craning over the bar, whispering in the bartender's ear and handing him a note. The bartender stumbled back surprised, crooked grin across his face, looking at his hand.

Toni hopped off the stool like a kid and bounded towards me, smiling and shaking her head. She scooped my elbow, walked me to the elevator and pressed the UP button. "What was that about?" I asked.

It wasn't a jealous inquiry. I didn't really know how I felt about Toni at that time. She was fun... a summer fling. But I wasn't her keeper. I certainly wasn't her boyfriend. We'd never had a conversation about being exclusive. In fact, we didn't have many conversations about anything.

The elevator opened and we stepped in.

Apparently when I went to the bathroom, the bartender stated emphatically: "that guy you're with isn't good enough for you. Let me take you out sometime." He wrote his phone number on a cocktail napkin and slid it to her across the bar. Toni grabbed the note and made a bee-line to the bathroom. After our porcelain quickly, she cleaned my ejaculation with *that* napkin and tucked it in her hand. While I was walking to the elevator, she took the opportunity to hand the napkin back to him.

She finished her story with: "I leaned in and whispered in his ear... 'I just fucked him in the bathroom.'"

Toni's eyes widened in surprise as her mouth dropped into a devilish O. As she backed away to gauge my reaction, she pressed her hands against the elevator wall and leaned on them in an impish pose – her head cocked to the side, her shoulders up to her ears – her eyes smiling, gleaming with delight.

I'm a man who is rarely rendered speechless, but that moment took my words away. I guess there was nothing really to say. I nodded my head and smiled. We stepped out of the elevator hand-in-hand towards our room.

The dark gray clouds that blanketed the island and soaked us with rain, eventually moved along. We lifted the thick hotel blankets off our cocooned bodies, pushed the room-service trays aside, split the curtains open, and let the air-conditioned room illuminate with sunlight.

We returned, reluctantly, to our regularly scheduled lives at the condos to chase the geese and paint the walls.

THE
P-38

The Greatest Generation was so named because in 1939 everyone on the planet either picked up a gun and went to war, knew someone who picked up a gun and went to war, or helped in the cause of getting people guns so they could go off to war. The criteria for being the greatest isn't very high, but a shitload of them died on the battlefield in the name of world peace, so they deserve some kind of recognition.

Man has been creating war since he crawled from the muck… or, appeared magically in the Garden of Eden. You choose which one to believe. When we weren't chomping on apples or slurping micro plankton, we were picking up weapons and massacring each other in the name of God, country and politics. Using spears, trebuchets and atom bombs.

The Greatest Generation hoped to be the last to fight a global conflict in which every boot hit the ground and every hill was either protected or attacked in our desire to be free – the ground seeped in blood from England to Australia.

Later, when the smoke cleared, the toils of war reconstruct-ed the men as smiling, determined entrepreneurs who secret-ly pounded alcohol to get through the day while their wives cooked hams in the kitchen in full makeup... who also secret-ly pounding alcohol to get through the day. This was deemed the American way. They pumped out a ridiculous amount of kids -- like a never-ending procession of B-29 Bombers drop-ping whistling 500-pound aerial bombs. They quickly repopu-lated the decimated numbers. A human baby "boom."

My grandparents were good, salt-of-the-earth people. Both of my grandfathers fought in WWII. My paternal grand-father Andrew J. Schmitz Jr. was a Lieutenant and stationed in the pacific with the U.S. Army. He worked for the OSS, the Office for Strategic Services – the precursor to the CIA, doing intelligence, counter-intelligence and code-breaking. In photos of him in uniform, he's lean and bony, as he would be through life, yet without his trademark black, broomy mous-tache, which made his bulbous nose (a trait that I would in-herit) more apparent. Unfortunately, he contracted Malaria and was shipped home. Surprisingly, the Malaria didn't really affect him much through his life... probably because he drank a six-pack of German beer every night, which kept it at bay.

My maternal grandfather was in the U.S. Coast Guard, also a Lieutenant, but, unfortunately, he didn't catch Malaria. He was one of the poor souls who stormed the beaches of Normandy on D-Day, June 6, 1944. But, Gerald Piffath didn't carry a gun... he carried a bag. After he dropped his fellow soldiers onto the beaches in long, flat-bedded 'Higgins Boats,' it was his task among many to clean those same soldiers off the beach. Piece by piece. It was a horrific act that haunted him through his entire life. Anyone curious enough, or brave enough, or perhaps *dumb* enough to ask him about it, got a steely glare that bore holes through their solar plexus, a gruff response of "I don't want to talk about it" followed by a stiff swallow of vodka.

We have black and white pictures of grandpa during his Coast Guard service. The first is a standard posed shot, chipper and youthful as he leans on a ship's Morse Code light communicator – a sailor's cap pushed back exposing his rounded forehead. He's chubby even then… full bodied and tall. The other photo of him is on the bow of a patrol boat, bundled tightly in a peacoat, foot up on the railing with a Reising M50 submachine gun resting on his forearm as he looks out over the water. He's a different man in this shot – a candid photo taken by a mate. His once rounded cheeks that rose high on the bone are now lower in the jowls. His thousand-yard stare with sad, darkened eyes had seen death a few times over. He's not acting tough in this photo – he *is* tough. World weary and unquestionably shattered.

My grandfather was a quiet man. He had a beautiful wife and five great kids, but his silence was different. He wasn't necessarily a quiet man by nature. I believe the war took a piece of his soul. He saw things that no man should see and he prayed to God and fought bravely so no man should have to see those types of things again.

Their service and bravery were undeniable, yet, most of my family's World War II glory went to my Grand Uncle Bill – a bona fide war hero. Uncle Bill didn't talk much about his time in the war either. That's because he didn't have to. It's well documented.

Lieutenant Colonel William Geiler was the Division Engineer & Battalion Commander for the 55th Armored Engineer Battalion, 10th Armored Division, Third Army. In layman's terms, the men who fought under General George S. Patton in his tank brigade as they rolled through Europe. *The Battle of the Bulge* and all that. The 10th Armored Division was nicknamed the Tiger Division. Their motto: "Terrify and Destroy" – and that's exactly what they did.

By the time William Geiler came home, he'd received a bronze star, a purple heart, two silver stars and enough pins, ribbons and medallions to tip a man over onto his face. His sitting den was a glistening trophy room, which fascinated anyone who entered. Besides a glass case filled with those medals, ribbons and medallions -- his knotted, shellacked, pine-lined walls were a museum of honorary plaques, proclamations and a tantalizing assortment of guns and knives collected along the way -- Broom-handled Mausers, Indian Kukri knives and a good old-fashioned American Colt 45.

He had a portrait of himself in dress gear on the wall, done in colored pastel by a German POW in Garmisch Partenkirchen, Bavaria in August 1945 after the war ended. An excellent use of a perfectly good German artist. The portraits gaze would follow you around the room with its steely, auburn eyes.

Uncle Bill's most prized "scalp" though, was a pair of Nazi leather riding boots, each strapped with a double-sided swastika dagger in scabbards that he fashioned into table lamps. A conversation starter for sure.

The craftsmanship of the Nazi materials was bar-none – incredibly well made and even beautiful in their design.

Uncle Bill would be the first to praise the Germans for their adroitness and expertise -- in weaponry and in war strategy. But that was, and is, the way of the soldier. They love to praise their fellow commanders in arms.

The generals of World War II fell all over themselves to praise their fellow enemy warmongers. Patton admitted to reading Erwin "The Desert Fox" Rommel's *Art of War* and Rommel returned praise of Patton, although less publicly. "Know thy enemy and know yourself" was the philosophy they adhered to all too well. Nothing works a general into a froth more than studying the brilliant war strategies of their fellow opposing generals. Sometimes these men would meet in undisclosed locations and kiss each other's ass over tea while their pawns died on the battlefield. Every scholar loves to talk about the brilliant tactics of Confederate General Robert E. Lee, regardless if he was on the wrong side of history or not. Sure, "Lee fought for South," they say, but good Lord, could that man dictate an offensive! After the generals and majors have time to reflect, in their wooden sitting dens or their lush garden vistas, they can heap praise on the enemy and their embattlements after the dead are buried. Especially if they're on the winning side. My Uncle Bill was no exception. His admiration for the Germans... their rigid loyalty to God and country, their razor sharp design aesthetics, bordered on fanaticism. You'd begin to wonder which side of the war he was on after he'd consumed a decanter or two of strong gin. He was German by blood after all – through and through. As we all were... some of us having accrued more percentages than others. His real name was Max William Geiler, but his mother called him Bill because she felt there was a stigma around Germans after the trauma of World War I, and the name Max might not be well accepted.

There was a lot of skepticism in those times, all the way through the cold war. Communists were such a threat, they held witch trials to weed them out. A German name or a Japanese face would receive leers that could cut. Although they had the moniker of Greatest Generation, they were probably one of the least tolerant generations. It wasn't just the red scare that crept into their lives. The Asians were trying to buy their land, the Mexicans were crossing the border, and the blacks were getting more freedoms all the times. They fought for freedom, but as long as their neighborhood lines were clearly drawn, they had no problems. They fought for freedom, but that freedom had rules.

•••

My Grandpa Piffath didn't have a trophy room, but his study did display a few war trinkets collected here and there. Beside some hand guns fastened to plaques, long-rendered dummies by having their chambers clogged with molten metal, he had a canvas bandolier ammunition belt, Uncle Bill's brown dress cap emblazoned with brass eagle pendant, and handfuls of spent bullet casings in various calibers -- small, medium and church-organ-pipe large. All of them given to me freely without question.

After my grandparents downsized to a small condo, Grandpa jammed most of his things in the attic above the garage. When I was around 14, I'd come visit and go up there and dig around. He never stopped me. He knew I'd find little treasures that would fascinate a boy my age, so I was free to roam. Whether he'd forgotten what was up there or he didn't care, I can't say, but the treasures were plentiful... especially plentiful for a man and his brothers who'd been to war. Sniper scopes, helmets and compasses too.

But the one true treasure that I'd longed to find was eventually uncovered. A German Walther P-38 pistol – in perfect condition – the premiere sidearm of Nazi officers during World War II. Gunmetal black with brown Bakelite handles that swirled in a pattern like coffee that was just hit with a little dab of cream, the heavy steel gun fit perfectly in the hand. If my Uncle Bill was a man who found much to admire in the mechanical craftsmanship of the German gunsmith, the Walther P-38 was atop the list of enviable items.

The gun was not only clean, but pristine. Still well-oiled without a hint of rust – each section hammer-stamped with matching serial numbers. I cocked the slide back and it locked in place with Swiss watch precision. The slide catch mechanism was comfortably near the thumb and one flick slid it back into place with a spring-loaded snap. The magazine clip slid out easily and clicked back in place like a tailor-fit glove. Holding it my hand, I got an immediate sensation of not only power, but history. My grandfather swiped it off a dead Nazi soldier on the beaches of Normandy and took it home. But not in secret. Many soldiers took guns home as souvenirs. The only stipulation for transport back to the U.S. was to cut the firing pin to render the gun useless. This P-38 was no exception. This gun would never fire again.

Walther was a German gun manufacturing company

founded by Carl Walther in 1886. They crafted exceptional firearms that are still made today. British Secret Service agent James Bond, AKA, 007 uses a Walther PPK, an accurate gun that conceals well. The sidearm of choice for the German Army for years was the Lugar, or Lugar P08 – the thick handled, skinny barreled, toggle-lock (cocking it by pulling it up) pistol that is well documented in Hollywood films. Originally produced by Austrian Georg Lugar for the Swiss Army, the Lugar found favor with Germany and became its official sidearm when the Mauser proved unreliable – often jamming. The Walther P-38 was developed and implemented into the German army en masse by the early to mid 1940s to replace the expensive Lugar. Primarily a gun of the German officer, the P-38 never had a wide-spread emersion into the German army and thus never became as common as the Lugar. The P-38 is a beautifully crafted gun... well balanced, comfortable, and extremely handsome in its design.

I knew once I held my grandfather's P-38 it would be mine. I stuffed it back into its brown leather holster, which was equipped with a second clip pocket sewn to the side, holding another clip. Also in excellent condition.

I wrapped the gun in an old t-shirt and stuffed it into an argyle suitcase that I'd been loading with the other items procured during my archeological attic dig.

Carefully navigating the suitcase down the rickety pull down attic staircase, I walked through the kitchen while my grandmother made spaghetti and meat sauce. I told them I was taking the suitcase and they nodded and smiled while Columbo solved another murder on their tiny kitchen TV.

That was that. No questions asked.

The next day I folded the proper crew into my new discovery. The rag-tag group of misfits I ran with, each with their own specialty. The A-Team. My buddy Bob Gilman and my best bud Chip Fusaro. All of us Gung-Ho and full of bombastic ideas, fueled by Rambo, Schwarzenegger and a host of B-grade war movies starring guys who looked like Chuck Norris and on occasion, was actually Chuck Norris himself.

We attacked home-made couch-cushion dummies with nunchakus, katana swords, and fist-fulls of razor sharp ninja stars. For Christmas, we all got gargantuan Bowie knives equipped with compasses in the stock and hollowed handles that held matches and survival sutures when we were inevitably harassed by the local sheriff and forced into the woods to live off the land and repair any flesh wounds caused by long vertical falls.

Bob's father was a Navy Seal in the Vietnam War – a quiet man, no more than five foot five. He was a tunnel rat in 'Nam… the guy who was handed a flashlight and gun and crawled into holes to flush out the Viet Kong. Bob Sr. taught us martial arts and a hundred ways to kill a man with our bare hands. It was no wonder we were all so Gung-Ho. Our grandfathers were telling stories of WWII and Korea, while or fathers and their friends recounted the fresh wounds of Vietnam. For Bob, the acorn didn't fall far from the tree. He was a weapons expert before he left Junior High. He could shoot any gun with marksman precision, could handle a knife in any combat situation and camouflage himself anywhere at any time.

But most important to my newly discovered handgun was Chip: a guy who was good with his hands. While Bob was unwrapping a Heckler and Koch rifle under the tree on Christmas day, Chip had been fashioning swords in his basement for a month on his new bench grinder – a gift he couldn't wait until December 25th to open. When not pulling scrap metal off his neighbors' garbage piles to bend into stabbing weapons, Chip was crafting crossbows, dart guns and because he was creative, the occasional puppet.

After Chip and I studied the P-38, we popped the indicator cover off the top slide to expose the mechanic workings. We carefully removed the firing pin, noting and documenting where all the springs, screws and latches went, so when it came time to put it all back together, we did it correctly. A thin, yet strong piece of steel, the firing pin resembled something like a lock-picking tool crossed with a skeleton key. It had grooves, a flat middle and two cylinders in the back and front end that slid into a guiding chamber – all fashioned from one piece of hard steel. We knew to replicate the pin, we needed the strongest piece of metal we could find. Hard and durable. Spring steel. The only place we knew to get spring steel was at a craft store down the street called Caboose. They sold everything from Marklin trains, arts and crafts materials, balsa wood, model airplanes, and everything you could twist into your favorite hobby. And of course, long pieces of spring steel in various thicknesses.

Chip and I hopped on our bikes and went to Caboose for spring steel... just two 14 year-old, All-American boys going into town so they can fix their handgun.

We brought the firing pin with us so we could find a steel rod whose circumference matched the gauge as closely as possible. To our surprise we found one that was dead-on to the caliber of the pin. So easy!

Unfortunately, we were not versed enough in our knowledge of metal to know that spring steel is INCREDI-BLY tough and extremely difficult to work with. Not only is it strong, it's virtually impossible to cut with mere household tools -- even ones made to cut steel. It's a metal that really needs fire to cut. So Chip and I spent hours trying manipulate it before realizing the only way to get the steel to do what we wanted, was to meticulously and painfully grind away the metal on his disk bench grinder. A task that would not only take hours... and days... but WEEKS.

Together, we tag-teamed work on the pin, day after day. I'd come and grind during the day and Chip would work at night, driving his mother crazy with the wheel's incessant whining. But eventually, we got it done. It wasn't perfect... we weren't German engineers after all... but it was good enough. As close a match to the original pin as two 14 year-olds using a stone wheel with inexperienced hands (that'd never even snapped the bra strap off a woman) could do. We set the pin back in the slide – springs and pins in their proper place – and set out to test the firearm.

But first, we needed ammo. That's where Bob came in.

Every once in a while, Bob's father would take the two of us out to a big gun store in the middle of Long Island called Edleman's -- a warehouse with row upon row, glass case upon glass case, of glistening, steely death contraptions. Chrome or black... snub-nosed or long-barreled, it had every-thing a firearm aficionado could want and more. Especially ammo. But to our great surprise, they wouldn't sell it to us.

This was a gun store with morals. We couldn't tell Bob's father to purchase bullets for us because obviously we'd have to tell him that we had a handgun in our possession. So we left Edelman's deflated.

But fear not! We went to a place right down the street called Arrows and they sold us bullets – no questions asked. Bob and I went right up to the counter and asked for a box of 9mm bullets, which the guy handed over to us 14 year-old kids like he would a pack of cigarettes! Sweeter still was the salesman. He was wearing a giant metal belt buckle that said BOB on it. When we told Bullet Salesman Bob that Bob was *also* Bob, it got a chuckle out of him that made us all as pleased as punch. It was like he was selling bullets to his own kin.

That was it. Deal done. Bob and I exited the store -- into the sunset -- with our generic box of live 9mm ammo.

The test firing came in the beginning of November. Right near my birthday. My parents always travelled around my birthday because they wanted to avoid giving me gifts. Kidding! They always gave me gifts -- then they got the hell out of town.

With the house to myself, Bob and I prepared to fire the P-38 in my basement. High on the list of our many concern, besides the integrity of a 40 year-old gun that was in storage since Hilter's last days, was the pin itself. In truth, we weren't sure if we'd made the pin-point where the end strikes the bullet primer, too long. We made sure it wasn't too short, that's for sure; but if too long, would it cause the bullet to simply explode? Bloat into a bomb inside the barrel and blast the P-38 into a wad of shrapnel? Turning my hand into a twisted stump? We didn't know the answers, but like two curious knuckleheads, we proceeded anyway.

To protect myself, I wrapped my body in old couch cushions. I'm not sure why, but we all seemed to have access to old couches. Probably because by the time we reached 14, we'd beaten the crap out of our parent's furniture and they could safely buy new sofas knowing we'd outgrown the desire to tear the new furniture to pieces. Besides, once something like a couch goes into the basement, it's pretty much halfway to the dump anyway. So they were free game to use as punching bags, fighting dummies and archery targets.

Bob lashed the cushions to me with rope from head to toe until I resembled a police bomb squad guy. The only difference between the bomb squad guy's outfit and mine was his being double thick, form-fitting, charcoal grey flax, and mine being red and beige, squishy-foamed, flowery rhombuses. If I was to lose my hand during this process, so be it, but I was not going to mangle any other part of my body. I was too young to be deformed. But, certainly not smart enough to think the process through. Not only did I pad myself with cushions, to protect my head and face, I wore a creature mask that I made out of foam, faux fur and leather, with rows of teeth made from painted rose thorns. Between the couch cushions and the mask, I may have been misconstrued for an apocalyptic man-animal with Vogue Magazine taste.

On a calm Autumn Saturday afternoon, we loaded a bullet into the magazine and slide it into the handle until it clicked into place. Wrapped-up tight like the Michelin Man, I pointed the gun at our yellow tweed couch pressed tightly against the white cement block wall.

Yes, we had ANOTHER couch in the basement. It was a 1970's couch-lovers paradise. Bob took shelter behind the remains of the couch I'd used for my bomb squad outfit, and I squeezed my eyes shut.

Of the Walther P-38's many features was the fact it was a double/single action gun, which means, you could fire the gun in one of two ways. The first way, single action, was to cock the hammer back and squeeze the trigger, which would release the hammer and fire the gun. Think of an old western revolver where they'd cock the hammer back and fire at a man in a dusty street. The second way, double action, was to have the hammer down (in the safe position), and squeeze the trigger, which would pull the hammer back AND release the hammer in one longer "double" motion – firing the gun.

When you cock the hammer of a gun back, the trigger moves back towards the grip as well. It requires much less effort to squeeze and fire. In some ways, it's a "hair trigger." Cock it back, and a light touch of the trigger can set it off... very easily. With the double action, the trigger is more forward, away from the grip and requires a good squeeze to get the hammer to cock back, catch, release and fire in one longer motion.

I decided that the double action was the right way to approach the test firing. Mainly because I didn't want it to go off while prepping myself to aim... either hitting a water pipe or Bob in the head.

So, with my vision and range of movement limited, I pointed the gun at the yellow tweed couch as Bob clutched the back of the flowered couch and ducked his head down.

I squeezed the trigger and BANG!

A deafening echo... the gentle clank of the spent shell bouncing on cement... a smoky haze... and my hand still attached to the wrist.

A perfect mechanical test.

Bob rose, I tossed off the mask and we ran to the couch. No signs of the bullet hole in the tweed mesh couch, so we hopped to the back. A small exit hole in the fabric, but a HUGE hole in the cinderblock wall. So large we could see through it and into the dark crawl space behind it. A clear shot!

Immediately we knew that every cop show on TV and every movie where the hero would dive behind a couch, or knock a dining room table over for cover as bad guys emptied their .357 magnums was complete bullshit. 9mm bullets are powerful, but not the world's strongest caliber. So our shock at the cinderblock's gaping hole gave us pause.

Inspecting the gun afterwards, the gun cylinder was back in the reset position. The P-38, like other guns, is blowback operated, where the bullet's exploding gas energy pushes the slide back to reload a new bullet as it slides forward again. Once it has fired its last round, the slide will lock back so all the shooter needs to do is push a fresh magazine into the handle and unlock the slide so it closes, chambers a bullet, and is ready to fire again.

I stuck my finger inside the open chamber and felt the hole where the pin would exit and strike the cartridge. I pushed my thumb against the back pin where the hammer would strike and pushed it forward. The pin head was already broken. That was it. One and done. All of our work to fabricate a new pin was gone in one ear-rattling crack.

Looking back, we probably should have forged it with fire and tempered it in water... but we didn't know such things at that time.

Poor Chip. He put so much sweat equity into the pin and never saw the P-38 fire.

After that, the gun became a simple showpiece again. I holstered it, put it in a white cardboard box with my grandfather's other war trophies and zipped it shut with multiple strips of wide drafting tape. I stuffed it in my closet, and there it sat for 15 years. Chip got married to his childhood sweetheart, had four boys and moved south. Bob entered the Army as an Airborne Ranger and did multiple tours of duty in Iraq. He was shot a total of nine times... and somehow, made it through. I moved to New York City and worked as an artist.

Years later, my father called me and told me to get all the boxes out of my old bedroom closet so he could put boxes of his crap in there. Every square inch of the basement was now full of stuff, and the last vestige of space was upstairs in my old bedroom closet. I took the train out from Manhattan with my girlfriend Sandy and she and I muscled multiple boxes back onto the Long Island Rail Road. I didn't own a car, and we couldn't get a ride, so the train would have to be our moving transport.

A few seconds after the train departed the station, I took inventory and realized we forgot a box. You can already guess which box that was. The box containing the Walther P-38. Not the box containing piles of nearly worthless comic books… not the box containing stacks of scratched records that I couldn't giveaway for free if I wanted to… and not the box containing painfully outdated clothing. But, the box containing an arsenal of WWII materials.

I freaked! I flagged the nearest conductor and told him I forgot a box on the station platform. He called back and it was immediately picked up by Port Authority Police and was on the next train behind us. No problem. Disastrously, that was after they looked through the box and found the P-38 and gave me a grim warning to meet them at the Port Authority Police station at Penn Station.

FUCK!

Sandy went home and I sat in the station for hours, surrounded by my boxes and waited for the verdict. The box was impounded, the P-38 confiscated and put into holding, and I was marked as a man who could be "potentially dangerous." Eventually, I was sent home.

After multiple phone calls to the police and other New York Transit organizations, I was told I could pick up my box of materials at the Hillside Facility: a LIRR employee support and train maintenance facility in Jamaica, Queens.

Inside the Hillside's dystopian block of beige bricks, I took ownership of my items. Everything, including the leather holster with extra magazine clip, was in there. The Walther P-38 was not. When I inquired about it, I was told I'd have to fill out paperwork and petition for its return to me. Since I had no original paperwork for it, I couldn't prove it was mine, my grandfather's, or anything more than something I bought off the street. It turns out it was never brought into the country legally, and as far as the U.S. Army and the New York Police

Department was concerned, it didn't exist. It was an undocumented, unserialized, untraceable firearm. A ghost gun.

After multiple rounds of frustrating, jaw-grinding phone calls, I surrendered to the fact that I was on a wild goose chase to nowhere. It was clear that not only was I *not* going to get my grandfather's gun back, but it was entirely possible the gun was lost, miscategorized... or, very likely, in the hands of a police officer who found it fetching and kept it for himself. The gun went from being a ghost, to nonexistent. Poof!

Not only was I deeply disappointed in losing the gun – but ashamed. My Grandfather took that gun off the beaches of Normandy. He was there, on one of the most famous days in American war history. Surely one of the most pivotal moments of World War II. I thought losing that gun was a slap in the face to me and my family.

But, as the years wore on, it dawned on me that the gun was just a hunk of metal. When I had the P-38 in my possession, a WWII collector offered me a measly $200 for it. He said they were common – not worth much more than what he was offering. The gun... was just a thing. The history of my family... that's where the real treasure was.

And speaking of treasure...

In 1945, as the aftermath of WWII began to settle, American forces established a headquarters in Garmisch, a beautiful Alpine town in southern Bavaria. Rumors and reports began to trickle in about Germans SS colonels hiding gold in the mountains. The Nazis, seeing the writing on the wall, began transporting massive amounts of gold from Munich and Frankfurt to the Bavarian Alpines while other high-ranking officials escaped to Argentina with gold, diamonds and jewels.

The high command sent a detachment of the 10th Armored Division Tiger troops, including my Uncle Bill - William Geiler, into the mountains to see if the rumors were true. And they were. The Tigers rolled up there and uncovered 728 bars of pure gold buried in the mountains. 270,000 ounces. Estimated price in 1945: $10,000,000. Today: $445 million!

Although there was rampant thievery happening with the Nazi gold, and by many accounts, much of the Nazi treasure still being unaccounted for, the Tigers loaded all the gold onto trucks and transported it back to the allied base in Frankfurt. They were given a receipt, with all the gold accounted for.

It's the basis for the film *Kelley's Heroes* starring Clint Eastwood, Donald Sutherland and Don Rickles.

When all was said and done, Uncle Bill received: a Presidential Unit Citation for "Extraordinary Heroism;" a Distinguished Service Cross; a Bronze Star; a Legion of Merit award; The Croix de Guerre – a French military honor for "acts of heroism" with a certificate signed by French General Charles deGaulle; and two Silver Stars – the second one pinned to his chest by General George S. Patton himself. When Patton saw that my Uncle Bill had already received a Silver Star, Patton hugged him and called him a "son-of-a-bitch" – probably the highest honor of all.

Their stories. Their service. The things they saw through their eyes. Both heroic and horrifying. The Walther

P-38 is long gone, but the memory of it remains. It's a representation of our forefathers and their part in history... a part of their story that can be carried down in the hearts and voices of their children.

Perhaps they do deserve the moniker of Greatest Generation. It's a hard designation to beat. Others generations deserve to be great too… Gen-X, Millennials and Gen Z, they're great too. We should all think of ourselves like that. Isn't that what our grand-folks fought for?

AWARD-WINNING WRITER

I'm an award-winning writer. Isn't that amazing?

An award-winning artist too!

I've won awards in graphic design, advertising, marketing and even a few Pollie Awards for excellence in political campaigning. I've won contests for poster art, contests for writing short stories and awards for sports as well. All of it completely and totally meaningless.

Of course there was a time when I thought it was meaningful. It's great to put on a resume. People lap it up like fresh cream. The context is irrelevant.

I'm an artist and I once came in first in a pie-eating contest. They gave me an award. So, I'm an "award-winning artist." Right?

I once went on a job interview and the interviewer asked me what awards I'd won and I told them truthfully I had no idea. They were shocked by this answer. They probably thought I had a list memorized of all my accolades but the truth was, I stopped caring at that point. Awards are great, and sure… gold statues and glass plaques are pretty, but my son can't eat them for dinner. You know what he can eat? Food… that I bought with money from the things I created that clients paid for.

There was a time when I did know what awards I won. I used them as some kind of leverage in the job negotiation process. It was like collateral.

"Here's five design awards I've won and perhaps that's enough for you to give me $10,000 more a year."

It's the same negotiation process prisoners use in jail except replace 'awards' with 'cigarettes' and replace '$10,000' with 'not getting knifed in the chest.' It's also how the white man got the island of Manhattan, and look how that turned out for all parties involved.

I gave up tracking awards when I realized that many awards are not won on a whim by independent bodies examining the best-of-the-best work. You must campaign for the awards. You must pay an entry fee and submit the works. It takes time, money and energy to do so. Sometimes, more energy than the time it took to create the work in the first place.

When I worked at HBO, we had an art director who spent half a year examining, categorizing and submitting our work to design award competitions. It was literally a full time job. While others were busting their ass creating work for the client, he was submitting entries to award shows so we could advertise that we won awards. We submitted so many awards in so many categories, we were bound to win *some* of them. The numbers guarantee it. If you put a thousand tickets into those little raffle bags at a local charity event, you're almost guaranteed to walk away with a gift basket or two, whether you want them or not. Sure, you dropped two grand for 200 worth of shit, but you WON!

My father wins stuff all the time. He's constantly throwing his name in a hat or donating something to charity and inevitably receives a phone call a few days later asking him to pick up whatever he won. Usually it's a gift certificate, but at times it's something completely impractical to him -- like underwater speakers, or $100 worth of engraving on the lawnmower of his choice. He then defers the winnings to me, and I show up to accept my wicker basket filled with energy-saving light bulbs or packets of pickling spices flowered around a $4 bottle of wine.

One time I won an electric power washer from Home Depot and I immediately turned around and gave it to my father as a Father's Day gift. I flipped the script. Plus, I figured they must be giving it away for free because the faulty rattle-trap mixes water and electricity. The company was probably buried under multiple lawsuits for electrocuting people. So, I gave it to my dear-old dad first to see if he survived. Once he did, I borrowed it and it's never really been returned to him.

When I worked at The History Channel, I won an award for packaging design. I believe I won the award a few times. The only way I knew we won the awards was when my workmate Katy's head popped over the wall of my cubicle like a puppet show and announced it to me with the enthusiasm of someone on hard drugs. There was a ceremony and everything... one in which I was not invited to. I think I won more awards, but as I said, I lost track. The award-winning items are rotting away in a box in my closet. I haven't looked at them in decades.

Being a huge film buff, my dream was to make a film and win an Academy Award. It was the most prestigious award any artist could win in any achievement on earth… so I thought. Now, I'm not so sure. I believe if I was nominated for an Academy Award, I'd be happy to go. They say it's great *just* to be nominated, which is something losers love to tell you. Even if they haven't lost yet. They say that knowing they'll most likely lose. It helps soften the crushing blow. But if I'm nominated, it means my achievement in film was recognized, and that's a good feeling. I assume Academy Awards are submitted for recognition as well. Just like everything else. Going to the Academy Awards means I'd have to do a bunch of stuff I'm pretty sure I gave up enjoying a long time ago, like wearing a tuxedo and schmoozing with people I don't know or like. I'm almost positive I don't want to be on TV and the truth is, sending another person up to accept the award on my behalf would be a trip. Maybe a Native American cyborg or Chris Rock.

The descriptions on the backs of DVD cases and every Rotten Tomatoes ad showcases the award-winning star of the movie. Sometimes they'll even tout the actor if they *almost* won an award. "Starring three-time Golden Globe Nominee Meg Ryan in a powerful performance of love and redemption." They'll even promote the obscure Oscar-winners most viewers hate seeing during the Oscars telecast. "Winner of best sound editing – *American Sniper*."

When you're a kid, winning awards is the best. A ribbon on field day is a thrilling achievement. All your days of running around like a maniac finally pay off in a ribbon that is clasped to your chest with a safety pin.

Sports trophies are good too. Kids deserve trophies for physical achievements in school. Once these athletes are adults and become professional players, the trophy is exciting, but they just want to make money. Have you seen what pro athletes are making? Some earn more money than third-world countries. I believe Patrick Mahomes could fund the military of every country that end in '-stan'

My parents have rooms full of golf trophies. It looks like a showroom for a crystal company... all engraved with their name. I'm not sure what they're going to do with all of those things. None of them are practical. Even though some are cup shaped, you can't drink out of them... and some are tray shaped, nothing can be served on them. I don't think they remember half the championships they played in. But, my parents don't play golf for a living.

The awards I'm associated with were things I did for money, so the money was my reward. I'm not sure why they were entered into award shows other than to tell people we were award-winners.

"From the award-winning team that brought you this poster... here's *this* poster."

When I was in high school I won an award for 'best recycling poster.' Got my face in the newspaper and everything. I felt a sense of pride, but in reality, other people helped me with the poster and they didn't get accolades and I was never sure why.

One day my workmate Gary asked me if I wanted to judge an advertising contest for a national energy contest and I said yes, and before I could blink, I was on the voting committee for six years in a row. Now *I'm* a judge and I'm the one who tells people if their work is award-worthy or not. People probably hate me because of it. I'm responsible for giving companies, and people, the title of award-winner. Hopefully they found it as meaningless as I do now. Just because something won an award doesn't mean it's the best. Right? When was the last time an album won a Grammy that was loved by everyone? There's so many genres of music I can't imagine everyone thought a rock album was the best album of the year when a large chunk of people listen to country, hip hop and soul.

The Nobel Prize is nice and it comes with a decent cash prize. Henry Kissinger won a Nobel Peace Prize like, five seconds after carpet bombing half of Asia, so I'm not sure if the criteria for winning is properly vetted at all.

The thing about awards is once you win one, people easily forget that you won one. Brad Pitt won an Oscar for best supporting actor in *Once Upon a Time In Hollywood*, but he already had an Oscar as a producer for *12 Years a Slave*. Now he has two Oscars. Brad Pitt has a lot of money and two Oscars. Which do you think he'd like more... no Oscars and money, or no money and two Oscars? I think we know the answer.

There's so many awards we can't keep track. There's People Choice Awards and Actors Guild Awards and about 35 different country music awards. People are dying to give out awards. If you're not careful, you could take a bad step off a curb and be handed an award.

In my most recent design office, we had so many statuettes they got in the way. When we downsized, the statuettes occupied a whole table – an army of little gold and silver men holding disks over their head... a gleaming *Battle of Bunker Hill* marching towards my desk... all covered in dust and dull from neglect. Every time I saw them I wanted to say: "Can someone sweep these awards somewhere?" None of our potential clients looked at the award brigade and shouted: "you're hired." They weren't swayed that easily. They wanted to see things like... oh, I don't know, our portfolio, case histories and success rates. Stuff like that.

Over the years I've submitted my writing to all kinds of contests. I won a one-minute screenplay contest. That was great, but they don't make one-minute movies and the win did not propel my name into the screenplay stratosphere. I've entered screenplay contests for comedy, science fiction and dramas. I never won any of them. The contest people won – my money. They probably didn't sell the screenplay that won the contests either. They're selling hope, not stories.

I write books, but I wasn't sure what the criteria for a Pulitzer Prize or a Hugo Award were. Do I need to submit something? Will someone just read my book and say, "wow, this needs to win a Pulitzer" and submit it for me? I'm sure a ton of people have read my books and instantly thought 'Pulitzer' but that doesn't means I'll win one.

After some research, one *does* need to submit a book to the Pulitzer Prize committee to win the award. So I did. The entry fee was $75. The Pulitzer won my money. Because they have a new category for memoirs, I submitted my second book *The Death of Our Dreams: And Other Funny Stories*. Did it win?

Of course not!

The books that win are uber-intellectual subjects about things NO ONE reads about. The biography subjects are so unique, you're not sure how anyone stumbled upon the subject to write about it in the first place. Scan the past winners and the titles are so long and complicated, they're practically books themselves. They have titles like: *Bombed Out – How I Survived a Nuclear Bomb Being Dropped on My Head* or *The 5,000 Rapes of the Mele Kalikimaka Tribe*. Humorous memoirs about my life don't win these types of awards.

When I logged in to listen to the awards announcement via live (recorded?) Youtube feed, I knew within seconds I was shit-out-of-luck. The woman reading the subjects and nominees sounded like a robot librarian on horse tranquilizers. It may have been an AI-generated bot doing the work. I couldn't really be sure. I came in late to the stream and the voice was in the middle of a mouthful of warbling stances... rattling off a lengthy title a few words shy of the Gettysburg Address. By the time she read the winner, I'd forgotten what I was listening to. It's the same mode my brain goes into when I'm confronted by a stream of banal information and large words – sleep mode. Not shut off mode... sleep mode. My brain is there, listening in the background, but doesn't fully awaken until the speaker's voice changes tone like it does when it's about to change subject, ask me a question, or in this case, announce a winner. Kind of like a computer. The screen is dark, but it's on... listening to your words and recording images of you naked... but doesn't awaken until you bump it with the vacuum cleaner.

Needless to say, I didn't win. I'm not sure who won. My disappointment was immediately replaced with apathy and a glass of wine. Again, a Pulitzer is great, but I can't use it to pay off my debt. It may help me sell more books, which does benefit me, but I'm not sure. Sometimes these awards have cash prizes and that's when things get really good. I've never won a cash prize.

Like I said, my father wins all kinds of things. I believe the reason is because he doesn't care if he wins or not. In fact, half the time he forgets he entered something. He basically tells the universe "I don't care" and the universe rewards him with stuff.

That's why gamblers never win. They're too dependent on the outcome. Their crazed, maniacal vibrations send energy into the stratosphere that is met with instant resistance. Put 10 grand on the New York Mets to win and you might as well toss that money right in the goddamn trash. Of course, no one should bet on the New York Mets, but that's a different story.

My son recently won a Dunkin' gift card, which he gave me, just like my father gives me his winnings. I'm benefitting from other people winnings. I suppose the "contest-winning" gene skips a generation. My son also has the "I don't care" attitude and the universe rewards him in kind. The Dunkin' gift card was for 5 bucks. Most people sniff at that kind of money, but I don't. Those five smackers got me a raging-hot cup of coffee and a jelly donut. Basically made my whole day. With that delicious coffee and sugary donut in my hands, I felt like an award winner.

An award-winning writer.

I'LL BE FAMOUS
WHEN I'M DEAD

When I was 25, I could pass for 18. When I was 30, I could pass for 22. At 28, I would get carded for cigarettes, a product that requires you to be 18 to stick in your face and light on fire. When I was 33, I would get carded for beer, a beverage that requires you to be 21 to vomit on yourself. Over the years I've always looked younger than my age. Now that I'm 51, I can pass for a man of 48. The gap is narrowing. The grey is setting in, but, so is the stress. Most of it financial. Eventually it will go the other way. I'll be 60 and look 70. A parallax view.

My youthful looks have a lot to do with genes, but also because I was fairly stress-free most of my young life. Not privileged, per se. More like clueless... not really paying attention to what the hell was going on. Living paycheck to paycheck was easier. An occasional bout of couch surfing was more tolerable. Procure a wife and kid along the way and the responsibilities mount... pile up... along with the bills, and before you know it, the hair is grey and the person you saw in old photographs; the one you thought wasn't very attractive when you were that person, is actually really good-looking. I've picked up my fair share of photos of myself on the beach or poolside and said "I was self-conscious about my looks? This guy is hot! Look at me now! I'm an old wreck!"

I've managed to stave off the wrinkles, but, it's only a matter of time before the crow's feet stamp their mark around my eyes like a fork in pie crust. As a guest on a recent podcast, the hostess stated that I looked around 32, which was the best news I'd heard all year. But, she based that on a profile photo. I believe if she saw me in person, she may have tacked on a decade or two.

I keep reading about how scientists may be able to "reset" the body clock and stop the aging process. They'll solidify those results on my deathbed. I'm not sure I want to stop aging. I don't want to die today, but I don't want to be a clunky bag of bones at 95. I'm not sure I want to live to the age of 200 regardless of physical and mental strength. I'm struggling to get by on the earnings of a man projected to die at the average age of 75. Who is going to hire a 188 year-old man? McDonald's? I'm over the summit and on the downward slope. At the bottom of the hill is an open grave. I can slide in safely with minimal issues at a ripe old age, or I can stumble in tomorrow. Fate will decide that, I suppose.

I'm not a decrepit old man, but I'm no spring chicken either. I feel like I'm 25, but the pain in my neck says otherwise. The point I'm trying to make here is, although I look pretty good, I'm not getting any younger. I won't live forever and time is running out.

My great fear in life is never achieving success – living a below-average life on a perpetual ride of mediocrity. I gave up my dreams of living any kind of romantic life long ago. That mansion I envisioned with two pools (one fresh and one salt water), has given way to a house that has a bathtub. I'll take a house with one bathroom. The shower can be a stand up. As long as water is being piped into the place on some level, I'll chalk it up as a win.

But a greater fear of mine outside of mediocrity, is a wildly successful career as a writer that comes long after I'm dead. What good is raking in the dough when I've been roasted into dust and sprinkled around the seaside of Long Island? I have a son and he can reap the benefits, but I'd like to enjoy the fruits of my labor as well. I'd enjoy a decent cut of steak that I don't need to rip with my teeth like a tiger tearing a leather shoe. I'd like to take a trip that brings me outside the borders of the town I live in. And maybe, just maybe, I could buy a house that has one of those bathtub things I just referenced.

According to Twitter... and not through statistics or analytics, but through observation... there's about 900,000 writers out there trying to make it. I'm one of them. I don't have the capacity to read 900,000 books a year, but I assume based on averages alone, a large chunk of them are terrible. Every writer thinks they're a good writer. I think I'm a good writer. There's 900,000 actors flooding into Hollywood every year and they're not all good because there isn't 900,000 movies being made by 900,000 filmmakers staring these 900,000 actors. I'm sure there's some really good actors who eventually leave town and become carpenters or work at coffee shops.

Decent, respectable jobs, all of them. But these jobs are not 'movie star' obviously. I'm sure there's some writers that are real gems out there too, trying to make it in a very difficult profession. They may jump ship before their finest work is ever written. They give up.

I don't plan to give up writing. It's all I do, actually. As I stated before, I can't afford to go anywhere outside of my town and I can't even afford a decent bathtub, so I write. I've been writing most of my life. Since I was 10. After a while, you develop some skills. Some muscles. But, it doesn't mean success. I don't believe in the afterlife or heaven, but maybe I should. It'd be nice to sit on a cloud and look down and say, "Look, that guy bought my book." I can then hop on another cloud and watch my son cash the check at the bank.

I recently picked up my first Charles Bukowski book from the library. I'd never read him before. After digging around on a book aggregator website, it sensed my miserable attitude and recommended Bukowski, so I picked up his first novel *Post Office*. I went down the Bukowski rabbit hole pretty hard. Although Bukowski was gaining some success writing poems and essays in small periodicals through the end of the 1960s, he didn't publish his first novel until 1971 when he was 50... the same age I was when I published my first book *Buggin' Out*. 1971 was the year I was born. So I began to feel a cosmic connection to him even though we lived on opposite coasts and in completely different times. By the time I became a man, he was already dead. He had some success, but his legend grew while he was in the ground. Like fertilizer.

Bram Stoker, born exactly 124 years before me on November 8th, didn't have his seminal work *Dracula* published until he was 50.

Vincent Van Gogh was miserably poor his whole life and suffered deep depression, killing himself at the age of 37. Self-portraits depict him as being a twisted older man of 50, but he didn't even sniff the 40-year mark. He created thousands of works, but never saw a second of success, and certainly never touched the millions his work fetches in today's ludicrous collectible art market. Sadder still was his brother Theo, who died six months later at 33, Vincent's biggest supporter.

Then we have probably one of the most delayed success story from a writer of all time. John Kennedy Toole. John wrote the masterwork *Confederacy of Dunces*, a book that won the Pulitzer Prize in 1981... 12 years after he committed suicide by asphyxiation when he ran a garden hose from his car's tailpipe into the window. His persistent mother pushed the book into the faces of every publisher she could find until Walker Percy took the bait and published it, garnering unmitigated acclaim and receiving multiple awards, including the aforementioned Pulitzer.

The problem with being a writer is the longer you write without any success, the more people stop believing in you. They drop like flies. Stop believing. Blow a cherry bomb off in your hand and whatever digits remain on your stump is how many people you can count on to still believe in you. It goes that way for just about every artistic profession in which the ultimate goal is money fueled and funneled by the attentions of thousands of fans. No one expects that sort of success out of ME. My parents weren't raised to be idiots. Movie stars and rock and roll singers were dreams for other people. Not us. By God, to waste any time dreaming of writing novels or painting pictures that people might purchase for cash is to think you'll fly to the moon and open a donut shop. It's ridiculous, heresy, and just plain delusional. A time-waster. Life would be better off tossing your dreams in the bin and getting a proper 9 to 5 job like the rest of the world out there. The rest of the sheep. All of them miserable and on the brink of death... their head under the guillotine and holding the rope with their own hand.

The 9 to 5 job... truly the deathblow to any and all creative inspiration, has culled many a great author from the heard. Anyone brave enough, or dumb enough to shun the working world and have a full go at the job of full-time writer is to live the life of great success or terrible tragedy. The term 9 to 5 is a phrase so vile and prosaic, to hear it is to see flashes of coffins before your eyes, whose interiors are nothing more than light grey drywall with fluorescent lights in their creaky lids. But, the drab office has its appeals. It's not the gutter... the literal gutter, where dirty street water and fecal matters runs and where Edgar Allen Poe was found in great distress and in need of medical attention. The poor bastard was a hardcore drunk and died soon after. It's been suggested he committed suicide or drank himself to death, but the cause is obvious... the dark and gnarled genius died of a broken heart. True, his wife died at the tender age of 24, which drove Edgar into a deep depression, but his lack of success as a writer surely drove him into the dirt. Thank god he didn't have a mind-numbing office job or the poor boozer laureate would have died years before his wife. Although under-appreciated in his time, today Poe has garnered literary influence far and wide. He began to see touches of success, but by the time he hit the gutter, it was too late.

Henry David Thoreau was also touched by some success, but none like he had long after he was dead. Like Poe, he too became an alcoholic, taking to drink after the death of his wife. If my wife dies before me I plan to become an alcoholic as well. There's something tragically romantic about the writer who finds meaning in a bottle after their loved one passes away and their written words find no home in the hearts of others. I was planning on becoming an alcoholic *before* my wife passes away, mainly because she's one of the many reasons I drink in the first place. But, she seems dead-set on getting me to the gym and stuffing me with vegetables, which counteracts some of the alcohol in my system. She's trying to keep me alive and so, perhaps, I should help her by tending to my own health, while wishing her good health as well.

Franz Kafka never married and had no reason to be miserable other than lack of success. Although not a drunk, his misery derived from being paranoid. He thought people found him mentally and physically repulsive and had a fear of sexual failure. All the good traits of a writer. Like the other writers noted, he found no real success in his lifetime, and what little was published during his time, found notoriety almost immediately after he died of Tuberculosis, and essentially starvation, when his throat closed at the age of 40. Although he instructed his friend Max Brod to destroy all his unpublished works, Max ignored his wishes and had the works published, eventually garnering Kafka world-wide acclaim. For some reason Franz burned over 90 percent of his works, which seems like a crime, but the man was obviously delusional... hence the word 'Kafkaesque' which derives from his bureaucratic, nightmare story backdrops.

Herman Melville had a small amount of success, but his book *Moby Dick* wasn't considered an American classic until almost 30 years after his death. He lived to the ripe age of 72 and although he had a silver spoon firmly planted in his mouth as a youth, he spent many of his adult years struggling financially, borrowing money from his family... something I know a lot about.

And then there's Sylvia Plath. Her seminal work *The Bell Jar* was published one month before her suicide at 30. Like Kennedy Toole, she died by asphyxiation, sticking her head in an oven until she was overwhelmed by carbon monoxide. She suffered from depression and possibly Bi-Polar Disorder. Also like Toole, she won her 1982 Pulitzer Prize posthumously for her work The Collected Poems, one year after Toole won his posthumously for Dunces.

Finally, we have Stieg Larsson, who wrote the *Millineum Series*, which include *The Girl with the Dragon Tattoo*, *The Girl Who played with Fire* and *The Girl Who Kicked the Hornet's Nest*. All of them international best sellers, turned into smash hit movies, and all of it presented to the world posthumously after Stieg died of a heart attack at age 50.

There's many more examples.

Had any of these people known what success might have come in the future, they may have hung on a bit longer, not only getting the financial support they needed, but the things that go with it like medicine and the obvious help of psychologists.

Still, there's a lingering ghost of fear in every writer that our work may go unnoticed in our time. Or even worse, found in its time and found to be terrible. For me, fame is of little concern. I'm more interested in garnering some notoriety so I can make a few bucks. Maybe send my son to college or get him a car that doesn't need duct tape to hold it together. Being famous could also mean getting soft. No more good writing. Maybe my anonymity and continuously stressful life is the fountain from which good writing springs. As Bukowski artfully stated: *As the spirit wanes the form appears.*

Every day that passes, there seems to be something that holds the attention of people's eyeballs that doesn't involve books. There's more streaming services than anyone knows what to do with, loaded with massive amounts of content to consume that to watch it back-to-back, would have you sitting in front of your TV for decades, if not a century. Not only that, there seems to be more writers than ever. So many people with a story to tell. Many writers who want their book in the world. But, does anyone read anymore? I assume so, because how does anything get done unless your read? Is it possible to read the amount of books coming to the market each year? Are they noticed? Are any of them good? Or special?

Most likely not. The only way to cut through it is to get lucky and be discovered, or, die and wait till the hands of time do their magic and present you to the world when you're dead and gone and can no longer provide fresh material to the fans enjoying your work – because you're dead!

Fat lot of good that does me.

THE STUPID
MACHINE AT THE GYM

You can find many Stupid Machines in all their magnificent glory at the gym, bobbing up and down on stupid machines. Sweating like pigs in the sun. Glistening like wet chrome. Pumping their muscles, fixing their physiques, sculpting themselves into Gods and Goddess. All of them pushing, pulling, dipping and bending while yanking on pulleys and cables. It's the ultimate fight against gravity. If people didn't want to sag so much, they should consider hanging upside down more often.

The gym patrons come in all shapes, sizes and mental disorders. The Muscle Heads, the Slim Runners, the Overweight and the Underweight. The Vain and Hopeless. The Cocky and the Cautious. All of them working to make themselves better. Better looking at least.

There's The Screamer, the guy who pushes the weights so hard he sounds like a banshee rising from the dead. In some cultures that's channeling chi… at the gym it's monkey noises.

Drop Everything Guy drops the weights so the entire gym rumbles like an 18-wheeler. He's HUGE and his ego huger. He walks like he's got balls the size of church bells and his lats are so wide, his arms stick out like someone hauling kegs of protein powder. He bangs into another HUGE gym bro and it leads to a showdown. The gym ain't big enough for the both of them. Neither are the walking lanes between the equipment. Something's gotta give. Medicine balls roll by like tumbleweeds.

Guys want to impress the girls. The girls want to impress the girls. Everyone checking each other out. The spandex tits, the padded asses, the penile packages. The men look too.

The gym is like a carnival funhouse with wall-to-wall mirrors. If you hit the right spot, you can contemplate your disappointing ass in real time. You can see your body from every angle and note what parts needs to be built up or reduced considerably. Usually it's all the parts.

The Bodacious Bootie Girls do dead-lifts, squats and anything possible to round their asses into gorgeous, buoyant beach balls. They have Tik Tok techniques and youth, which rival Kim Kardashian, but more importantly, they have big butts already. If they can't get satisfaction at the gym, plastic surgeons will do a life-threatening cosmetic procedure whose results will dissipate in a few years or devolve into some sort of cottage cheese quagmire. Sometimes they have a dangerous implant inserted that will flip inside them resembling the concaved part of a Frisbee.

Super Spunky Girl bounds around like a social butterfly. She's there for the networking engagement. She chats and talks, and once in a while does something resembling exercise. Somehow she's in shape already. She's the type of person who gets full eating ONE cookie. People hate her *and* like her. She's covering up her crushing depression and loneliness.

There's the 9-Months Late crowd. That's the delusional faction who started working out in May to be ready for swimsuit season in June, then came to the sobering realization that they should have started working out in May of *last* year. Three weeks on a treadmill won't melt away three years of bacon cheeseburgers with extra gravy fries.

Speaking of sobriety, Former Drug Addict hits the gym, but still wears Converse All-Stars and sleeveless Megadeth t-shirts. He has yet to go to the sporting goods store to get proper workout gear. He wears different colored socks and maybe even shaded sunglasses. He has bad tattoos, an ironic moustache, and a fringe of green hair at the end of his grown-out locks that are hanging on to their last, dying breath and will most likely be gone by his next haircut.

The gym can be as addicting as any drug. The endorphins, the routine. The good feelings. A place to go. It's like a bar, only these people are moving instead of sedentary and guzzle amino acids instead of booze.

The Old Men of the gym... they don't care. I mean; they do NOT give a shit. They lift weights to stack a few more years onto their lives, they're not there to impress anyone. They've lived. Their balls are dangling half an inch above the ground. I know this because old men seem to love prancing around the locker room naked. They shower and they're free. Free of inhibition. The old women too. They strike up a conversation like it's cocktail hour except they're naked and their tits are resting on their bellies like a couple of fried eggs.

Older Stupid Machines can't wait for the equipment to free up. They're in rush. They need the equipment before they die. "How many set's you have left?" is a popular question, even though the person on the equipment is in the middle of their first muscle squeeze having just sat on the device two seconds ago. "Three sets" they'll respond and the Older Stupid Machine will stand next to them and hover; count the seconds like a 100 meter dash.

On the opposite spectrum are The Teens. They swarm in packs. One of them moves and the others follow like a mumuration of birds swirling in patterns in the sky. All of them glued to their phones.

A lot of patrons are on their phones. They come in, do a few sets, then watch YouTube. They could do that at home; but why not do it on exercise equipment people want to use? Makes sense. People like having conversations on the phone. They're yelling, laughing, firing their employees... catching up with long-lost friends. It gets a bit out of control. The workout high is kicking in and they're yoked while yucking it up with someone who's most likely at a bar.

Overweight Guy is self-conscious – like everyone is looking at him. Because they are! Surprisingly, they're not judging. Just about everyone is secretly rooting for him. They don't want him to quit. But, the big guy will never know because no one talks to each other at the gym unless it's to ask how long they'll be on a piece of equipment.

"You using that?" is another frequent exchange.

The responder either nods or shakes their head, depending on the routine. Some people simply get out of the way. Most people are listening to music in their own little world. You ask them if they're done and they'll drift away to another spot.

Some Stupid Machines like to work out in the morning. They're up at the crack of dawn, eating, making deals and pumping iron. They do more before 9:00am than most people do all day. These people also need to nap at 2:00 in the afternoon. They're wiped out. The Stupid Machine can't go more than a few hours before it needs to rest. Especially after it's woken up and burned all its quality energy at the gym. Afternoon gym patrons burn off work stress. They hit the weights so they don't hit their bosses in the face. Instead of screaming into the air while their co-workers cower in fear, they scream into the air while lifting weights. The other gym patrons think it's so they can push the weight over the top like The Screamer, but it's actually the rage call of a thousand hours of office stupidity.

Nighttime Folks have jobs that require them to live on the edges of society. They work from 9 to 5, but when the moon is out. Night owls workout at 11pm, eat lunch at 3 am and are drinking whiskey when most people are drinking coffee.

There's so many different kinds of Stupid Machines at the gym. It takes all types. There's Vintage Guy. He's a lot like Former Drug Addict guy, but different. His striped knee socks were purchased on purpose and are up to the edge of his ball-hugging shorts. He's wearing a head-band like the 1975 Harlem Globetrotters. Not sure if he's clueless or doing the look because he saw it in ironic videos.

There's Fashion Girl. She's in shape, but wearing thousands of dollars in workout gear that's as stylish as it is impractical. Hoop earings, over the shoulder tops, side pony-tails, and gold leg-warmers are for 1980's Jazzercise videos and not 300 pound squats.

There's the Sweaty Guy and Girl – buckets of sweat pouring off them like a broken tap. More water out than they can get in, leaving every piece of equipment dripping with funk. THEY'RE NOT LIKE WATER GUY WHO IS WALKING AROUND WITH THE GALLON JUG OF WATER. Water Guy never gets thirsty. We know hydration is important; but a gallon of water? Is he living in the gym? Is there no other water sources anywhere? Is he using it as a free weight when his desired dumbbell is being used?

There's the Gentle Giant. Massive in every way – including his heart. People are intimidated by his size. He looks like a killer but wouldn't hurt a fly. He doesn't say much, but sometimes he'll give free advice about form and posture. Maybe a new exercise to try. The Gentle Giant is either dumb as an ox, or brilliant. You may never know. They won't speak because they went full introvert from relentless bullying at the age of 12 or they have a speech impediment.

The Stupid Machine is an amazing physical animal… so they say. You can spend three months at the gym killing yourself for some muscle definition, but take a week off and the body returns to a limp rubber hose. You'll need another three months to make up for that lost week.

Some days the gym is packed. Other days empty. Is it the moon? The weather? The rotation of the earth? The quiet gym can be like a library, lulling the patrons into a slumber.

The crowded gym creates an atmosphere of competition. The energy of the people can push other Stupid Machines past their normal weight tolerance. Most Stupid Machines lift too much weight. They see a guy three-times their size curl an 80-pound dumbbell, so they try and curl a 90-pound dumbbell. Their arm almost tears away at the elbow requiring 15 ligament operations, but as long as they don't come across as a pansy, everything is fine.

Some days everyone is on the equipment you want to use, and some days there isn't enough you to use all the free equipment. The Stupid Machines come in waves, like animals to a watering hole. One day everyone is doing legs, the next, on the bench presses. No one knows why. It's an interesting phenomenon.

A lot of Stupid Machines do floor work. On the mats. They're on their backs, flapping their legs around like a synchronized pool dance routine. They're standing on rubber balls, lying on rubber balls, throwing rubber balls against the wall or holding rubber balls above their head while squatting. Some balls are heavy and some are light. There's equipment you'd find in a ship yard – massive ropes to flap, or a huge truck tires to flip. If you decide to quit your job, you can work the docks of a cruise line.

Most gyms have classes.

Spinning Classes are bikes that don't go anywhere. You get all the boring exhaustion without the benefit of visiting new places. Perhaps the biking community stopped gyms from calling them biking classes because to bike means to have forward momentum.

Step Classes are the same. All the excitement you get

from climbing the stairs except you stay in the same place. The Stairmaster has the same philosophy, although you can watch TV while doing it.

Pilates is a lot like the synchronized swimming thing people do on the mats, except you're doing it with an ironing board and rubberbands.

Kickboxing is for those who can't lift their leg more than a few inches off the ground but still try anyway. It's a good cardio workout if you don't need a hip replacement afterwards.

Zumba is a combo of dance, martial arts and aerobics. There's throbbing music and sweating and it's similar to a Friday night out with the girls except there's no alcohol involved.

All of these things can be done while a Stupid Machine is yelling in your face. That's called a Trainer. You pay them money to yell at you. They'll yell at you on the bike, yell at you on the floor, yell at you while rubberbands are tangled around your neck, or yell at you while little 3-pound weights are in your hands. Sometimes they yell at you on the weight equipment. They'll command you to do "three more" and you stare and think: "If I do three more reps I'll fucking die!"

If you can't handle all the yelling, crashing, and throbbing beats, try Yoga. That's basically 50% exercise and 50% sleeping… all while twisted into a pretzel. It's where the Stupid Machine can escape from the grunting beasts, the clanging weight plates, the splashing sweat, the cell phone zombies, and the round neon asses shaking in their faces.

If one decides to quit the gym, good luck getting them to cancel the membership. It's a contract more iron-clad than Satan's soul-selling pacts. It requires 15 levels of authorization and at least a month on the phone screaming into the ear of someone that is most likely a computer. Angry emails go to a box that hasn't been monitored since Truman was in office, and you can watch helplessly as your bank account is charged monthly without recourse. It's enough to inflame you to the point of rage, and the gym is the perfect place to blow off that kind of steam.

PRICE
POINTS

For some reason, the culinary world is trying to force potato skins on us – the worst part of the potato. The fluffy interior tastes like anything from dry wall plaster to pure heaven, depending on your preparation method. You can scoop the potato from its shell and make creamy mashed potatoes, shred them for potato pancakes, shave them into disks for potato chips, or you can toss them in the oven because you're too lazy to do any of those things. Once removed from the oven (6 hours later) you can split them open and drown them in butter. Some people open the baked potato, take all the ingredients out, whip them with creams and cheese, and place them *back* into the skin and bake them again (for 2 hours). That's a twice-baked potato. If you want to eat it for dinner, it's best to start prepping it at breakfast.

In the 1970s, 1980s and a good portion of the 1990s, potato skins were a staple on the appetizer portion of a menu. I'm sure they still are in many places... places where beer is served in pitchers and cheese is on 99% of the items. I'm not sure who invented 'tato skins' but they were basically a genius. A master chef said: "What are we going to do with all these russet potato skins? The part of the potato that actually tastes WORSE than the sack the potatoes came in?" Then the chef's assistant, probably someone with an IQ lower than plankton or higher than Einstein said: "Let's fill them with cheese and serve them to drunk people." The chef tried it and it was a smashing success! Then he sent his assistant down a garbage chute, never to be seen or heard from again so he could take credit for the amazing 'tato skin' invention.

Although all the rage back in the day, potato bars are not as popular as they used to be. Again, some chef said: "how can me make profit from this 900 pound sack of potatoes they accidentally sent us?" Again, their plankton/genius-level assistant said something to the tune of: "Let's put cheese on it" and before they could grab a peeler, they presented a buffet featuring four kinds of shredded cheese, bacon bits, sour cream and 50 other foodstuffs to sprinkle on the potato. Then the assistant went to check on their bacon supply in the basement and was never heard from again.

Somehow, they managed to take a potato, which is worth about 2 cents, accompany it with 2 dollars-worth of heavy toppings, and charge people 12 bucks for it. The beauty of the potato bar is people go in thinking, "Wow! Endless potatoes for 12 bucks? I'm in!" then realize that most humans, regardless of their body mass index, can only eat one and a half potatoes. A hippopotamus can barely gulp down two. That's because potatoes are incredibly filling. There lies the genius of the potato bar and the profit margin. Eating two potatoes is like swallowing an inflatable kiddie pool – with water still inside. This is also the allure of the All-You-Can-Eat pasta deal. How many bowls of pasta can most people eat? I'm a pig and I eat one bowl of pasta and I feel like I ate a cannonball. Two bowls is equivalent to eating the actual canon itself – the kind they had on those old wooden ships that took six men to push through the port in the side. People march in thinking they're going to eat 15 bowls of pasta. Have people eaten pasta before? What lunatic thinks they're eating endless bowls of pasta? It sounds like an offer you can't refuse but trust me, you should refuse it. Maybe the mafia's involved. Or the Illuminati. Either way, it's a win-win situation for the restaurant biz.

Move ahead a few years later and we have the potato skin. If you've never eaten a tato skin, it's a halved potato, with the high-quality interior scooped out, leaving nothing but the dry, tree bark-like exterior that would normally require four or five beers to choke down your throat. Basically, the part of the potato most people have been tossing in the garbage or feeding to hogs for the past 5,000 years. So right off the bat, you have what is considered a negative food item. To get it back to some form of respectable, edible consumption-level, you need to load it with artery-clogging condiments. Sides. Sour cream, shredded cheese, chives, bacon bits, gravy, ranch dressing and anything else that helps this wooden boat slide down your throat. Eventually the toppings help it gain a net positive. That's why they're called 'loaded' potato skins. What else are you going to do? Dab that dry slab with a pat of unsalted butter? No! People need to get their money's worth. If there was a tray of salamanders and a bucket of toilet brushes, people would put that on their potato skins too.

This is a lesson in ingenuity. They took something virtually worthless and made it a delicacy. I use the word delicacy very loosely. Sure, it can be eaten with your mouth, swallowed and digested, but in reality, it's not really meant for that purpose. We don't eat the cardboard box crackers come in. It tastes like shit and has been man-handled by dirty factory workers, filthy machines, and cum-stained stock boys with hands like a level-5 germ warfare lab. The same with a potato skin. The potato, like the orange or banana, comes with its own packaging. We don't eat orange skins... they smell like oranges but taste like wet t-shirts. Same with potatoes. They smell like potatoes, but taste like newspaper.

Still, I commend them on their tato skin ingenuity. Think about the chicken wing – a nearly worthless, bony, veiny appendage with nary a shred of meat on it. Somehow it was turned into one of the world's greatest snack foods. You'll find them on any appetizer menu. Sometimes the restaurant is so prestigious the wings have their own section on the menu, in a box, with a list of sauces they toss them in. They have names like *Jack Daniels Glazed Rub* or *Smokehouse Five*. Sometimes they'll have the level of heat you can endure while eating them... some kind of scale that goes from the lowly 'wimp' level to the advanced 'asshole on fire.' I love wings and eat them by the cage full. But no one was going ape-shit over chicken wings 60 years ago. At some point a chef in Buffalo, New York said: "I've made 900 pounds of chicken salad, what am I going to do with all these wings?" and her assistant (who mysteriously vanished) said "Let's deep fry them and toss them in this sauce that tastes like a cross between Asian hot ketchup and an aluminum can." Thus, the Buffalo wing was born and the world forever changed.

Now wings are more precious than any part of the chicken. People size up a hen's value in relation to anything besides its breast. Like people who have foot fetishes when the ass is RIGHT THERE to be admired. For a while, breast meat was at an all-time low in popularity while wing prices soared – which is ironic because chickens are flightless birds. The prices go up during football season when the fans come out of their summer slumber, put on their football jerseys and scream at the television. This requires a lot of energy and wings are an excellent source of protein. At one point distributers were forcing wing places to buy breast meat so they weren't hampered with meat while shipping off the piddling wings by the truckload. Maybe that's why whole-cooked chickens are so cheap. Why are roasted chickens so cheap? Go to the grocery store and they're practically giving them away. A chicken in every cart! It's a great deal. At Costco they're like 4 bucks. They're cheaper than a toothbrush. It may have more mileage than a toothbrush. You can eat the chicken for dinner, make chicken salad for lunch and use the carcass as a football in the yard.

•••

Speaking of toothbrushes, why are they so expensive? It's a plastic stick with other plastic sticks sticking out of it. How hard can it be to manufacture these things? Why are they 6 bucks? I realize nothing is free; but 6 bucks? Are they made of diamonds? Rare plastic from the arctic circle? Is the Illuminati involved? I just got an email the other day inviting me to join the illuminati and although I was intrigued, I believe it was a fake email. I believe the illuminati recruit people in other ways, not by mass email. You need the bloodline of Jesus or something to join... not some random schmuck off the street like me. Maybe they're part of Oral-B. Have you heard of Oral-A? I didn't think so. Maybe Oral-B wiped them out... like a gang turf war. For all we know there was an Oral-C through Z and after the dust and gunsmoke settled, we had nothing but B. It's a vicious and unsettling business. One that requires nerves of steel and teeth like a bear trap.

I'm sure the toothbrush people don't like it when customers question the pricing of their brushes. They'll present an itemized list of all the things that make a toothbrush so damn expensive. Plastic infused trays, stamping machinery, packaging and other petroleum-based information I'll never understand. Not to mention union costs, insurance and lab testing. I can't even get into all the proper sterilization that quickly raises the price of their mouth washing sticks.

Sometimes I go to some dollar store and get five toothbrushes for a dollar. They come in these giant blister packs that someone stuck onto an aisle endcap, no more prestigious than Chapstick or a pack of mint gum. So I know someone's jacking up the prices of these toothbrushes I see at the pharmacy. The cheap toothbrushes I buy have absolutely zero bells and whistles. There's no angles, no fancy bristles, no neon colors or futuristic aerodynamics. It's a stick and to get to those tough mouth angles like back teeth and upper gums, I need to raise my arm or stick out my elbow, like most people have been doing for the past 500 years.

Speaking of Oral-B, I have an Oral-B toothbrush that's fancier than a car. It has swooping sight lines and strange and wonderful angles. It looks like an Olympic stadium from the future, the bristles being the part where the Olympic flame is ignited for all to see. It has angular, open holes – jutting, swooping prongs – a grip handle with about three different kinds of nubs, making it impossible to lose control when wet. The head has bristles on the edge running one way, and bristles on the other edge running the opposite direction. There's a trough in middle of the head for the center of the tooth and finger hairs that work the outside and massage the gums. Some of the bristles are dark blue, some are white, while others have a neon green tinge that spike from the side like bamboo shoots. This brush supposedly gets into every crevice of our complicated mouth cavities.

On the TV commercials, these brushes are destroying food particles like some futuristic exterminator. They can't even get actual footage of the mouth while the brush is in motion because the brush is creating a whirlwind of foaming madness. The simulation is animated, a computer generated cartoon, representing what each massaging bristle is doing to your tooth as it escorts broccoli and crumbs out of your mouth like white blood cells ridding toxins from the blood stream.

Dental floss is a high-priced item as well. It's string. That's it. How much can it possibly cost? Go to any Home Depot and for a few pennies you can get enough string to wrap the earth several times. Make it super skinny, coat it with wax and suddenly it's worth its weight in plutonium. I suppose they present it as a stellar item that requires a prestigious price. It's wrapped in a coil on a tube hub inside a little plastic home that you yank out and cut on a fancy little metal fingernail. If it's a super sophisticated floss, the plastic house has a little window so you can see the floss spinning around. Apparently this kind of sight-line requires money. One time I bought cheap floss and it was the same shit they use to rope cattle. I thrust it between my teeth and it felt like someone split my tooth with a hatchet. My wife was angry I bought the cheap stuff. Not only that, it wasn't waxed, which made it worse. By the time were done we had rope burn. Certain things should be lubricated to do the job and dental floss is definitely one of them. That rope floss is still in our cabinet, used only as a backup emergency. I fork it into my face and I remember why it's the 'backup floss.' It's better served in a tackle box to wrangle trout from a lake.

Sometimes we get those little floss hooks. They look like mini one-stringed lutes that someone might strum in a garden. You buy a bag and know immediately that the whole thing will be in a landfill in a few days. These lute flossers have a toothpick point at the end that can do all sorts of damage to your gums if you're not careful. I assume the knife end can be used as a lethal weapon in case you're jumped by gangsters or as a shiv when a gaggle of prisoners who've taken a disliking to you surround you in the showers.

4 out of 5 dentists approve this stuff and it's clear they've all been paid off by the higher forces at work in our government and possibly other influential organizations – like the illuminati. Or the stone masons. Or perhaps the American

Dental Institute. Who are these faceless doctors of the dental world? Why is there one dentist who doesn't want to agree with the other four? Do they know something? Did they not get their hush money? Are they getting money on the side from someone else... like Hershey's? Did Trident, the chewing gum company not offer them a case full of money, delivered at a cheap motel like the hitmen in *Pulp Fiction*?

In the 1950s, 4 out of 5 doctors approved Winston cigarettes for their patients who smoked. Especially the pregnant women. So, maybe the one doctor (or dentist) who didn't agree with the others knew something. Maybe they saw the writing on the wall and tried to help the world. Unfortunately, the illuminati got them and they're at the bottom of the sea wearing cement shoes and sleeping with the fishes and all that Jazz. Probably floating down there with the executives of Oral-P and Oral-T and the mysteriously missing chef assistants. It's a terrible cut-throat business.

My son has one of those fancy waterpiks – a shooting water gun that you stick between your teeth. It cost more than my car. It's fancy. It blasts food particles from your gums like the duck hunt game at the circus arcade. It has so many settings, I'm not sure you could explore them all in one lifetime. It has pulses, vibrations and massagers. It's like a garden hose nozzle for your mouth. It glows blue and looks like something James Cameron might drive to the ocean floor to grab footage of the Titanic. My son's oral care system costs thousands and I'm rubbing my teeth with a dollar's worth of cheap, unwaxed plastic. With the invention of 3D printers, we could probably print own toothbrushes and dental floss.

•••

Speaking of printers, why is printer ink so expensive? Have you seen the size of the cartridges? They couldn't possibly hold more than .0001 ml of ink in them. They're no bigger than a pack of chewing gum. The kind the 4 dentists approve of. The ink costs almost as much as the printer. They call them 'inkjet' printers because the ink costs the same as jet fuel. If you rerouted the money from ink cartridges into jet tickets, you could travel the world a few times over. Instead of printing pretty photos of beaches and mountain vistas, you could go and look at the places where the photo was taken with your very own eyes.

These days, companies expect you to print your own stuff. They send paperwork by the stacks and say "here, print this out and send it back." ME? Why do I have to print this crap? By the time I'm done I'll need to buy another cartridge of black ink. My son's school wiped their hands of all responsibility and said "here, you print all these required forms." It's going to cost me hundreds of dollars to get my son to play sports. Even though the school has a printer the size of a cargo container and can print thousands of documents a second, they want me to print on my inkjet printer that wheezes out a print every 8 minutes and costs me about $57 a side.

I bought my printer intending to print art and fun collages but I just print all the documents doctors and lawyers are too cheap to print for me. I print exciting things like immunization records for my son's summer camps, Boy Scout forms to fill out for enrollment, and insurance forms so I can be fully covered in case of accident or death. The sheets tend to drain one color more than the other… cyan for some reason, and then I have to buy another cartridge or the printer stops working. Maybe it drains cyan because most medical records are blue, like hospitals themselves. Perhaps that's a sterile color that represents cleanliness or recovery. Seems unfair for the printer to shut down when one color is empty. Maybe the printer companies are working with the medical companies, hoping you fly into an aorta-popping rage in the middle of printing your life insurance plan, unable to obtain coverage because you're dying on the floor, saving the insurance companies thousands of dollars. I wouldn't be surprised.

I don't care if my documents are in black and white, sunny orange, or a funky green. As long as I can complete the printing task at hand, they could be neon pink. If I run out of ink, it takes me forever to buy more. I usually need a small bank loan to pay for it. The loan requires paperwork, which I cannot print. It's a vicious cycle of corporate red tape, another color I don't currently have in my printer.

My printer has a series of numbers to identify it. D-780. The company only makes about 10 printers. Can't they be 1 through 10? Is the 'D' really necessary? Did they eliminate the 'A' series? Was the illuminati involved in this? Are they in cahoots with the Oral-B people? What does D stand for? Printer starts with a P and Ink starts with an I. I can't imagine what D represents other than Dick, which is what they give you in the ass when you're in the middle of printing and the ink runs out.

And what about 780? God only knows what that could possibly mean. Is that the size of the contraption in cubic centimeters? Its weight in gold? I only ask because when I have to get new ink, I need to match the ink number with the printer number. But for some reason the ink number is a completely different number. The ink is something like 401. What the hell does that mean? Like, 401K? What you'll need to cash in to pay for it? Can't the printer ink be the same number as the printer? D-780? Even better, can't the printer number be 2 and the ink that matches it be number 2 as well? What if the ink cartridges are the same for all 10 printers? Wouldn't that color our grey worlds nicely?

I've been tempted to get off-brand ink cartridges, but my printer won't cover the warranty if the fake cartridges screws up the machine. The fake cartridges are zombie cartridges that have been injected with new ink and tape slapped over the hole. It's big business. It's about 2 dollars cheaper, but hardly seems worth it. Knowing my luck, the printer will detect foreign substances and reject it, forcing me to either call a repair person, or simply toss the printer out the window and buy another one.

Even worse, I may be confronted by the repairperson who could be judgmental or even worse, work for the illuminati.

"So, you used off-brand ink, huh? Was that a wise decision you think? Why not just jam a potato in there and call it a day; hmmm?"

I'd be forced to confess… face the error of my ways and apologize. Promise not to do it again. As punishment, the repairperson will run a few ink-killing "test prints" through my printer. Those color bars and grey tone comparisons. They'll hand stacks of them to me… these worthless test prints, then immediately leave in an unmarked van with strange symbols on the side. Symbols like eyes in triangles, hands draped in rosary beads, and a giant letter B.

I'll consider myself lucky I wasn't tossed in a rotting ditch under a pile of potato skins with chefs assistants, the fifth dentist, Oral-C through Z and the poor bastard that sold me those cheap, imitation ink cartridges.

STARK
REALITY

When Andy Warhol stated in 1968 that everyone would be famous for 15 minutes, I don't think he could have imagined some of the neckless dreck that would parade across our TV screens today. Or, maybe he could. That's why he said it. Andy, as well as someone like filmmaker John Waters had an affinity for strange, unusual and even disgusting people. They can make good company and add sparkles of color to the brutally beige world we live in. I've been known to keep company with my fair share of cutthroats, scabs and disenfranchised louts in my day. I once hung out with a guy named Cliff who was a human kewpie doll of a man. The hair on the sides of his baldhead shot out like clouds. He rarely bathed and his cackling laugh made Tom Hulce's chuckle in the film *Amadeus* seem like the giggle of a modest Japanese girl. Because Cliff didn't have a telephone, the only way to communicate with him was through email, which in 1993 was pretty radical. He never knew where his next meal was coming from and a clock was something others used to be where they needed to be on time. One day he disappeared and I never saw him again. Poof! Gone, like a magic troll.

I guess this could be considered slumming it, for all intents and purposes. Spicing up a white-bread life with a collection of kooks and maniacs, knowing full well you can pull the parachute any time when it all goes terribly wrong. Keeping company with riff-raff, vicious freaks, drug vacuums and lunatics is all well and good until the car veers dangerously close to the edge. You look up, and not only is no one manning the steering wheel, everyone's in the back seat with you. There's usually time to open the door and step out when things get too weird and dangerous – even if the vehicle is still in motion. There's always another town to set up shop when the collection of crazies you've given a copy of your house key start taking over your life. Then you grow a beard, cut your hair and change your wardrobe along with your address. They won't likely find you. They'll eventually cling to someone else… like a crawling mold that forms around a ripe piece of cheese.

Some of these people can become your close, personal friends. Your tolerance of their questionable activities may vary. These people are free to shit in your yard as much as they want, but as soon as they shit in your hamper… all bets are off. Warhol and Waters called these kinds people family… "my kind of people" they'd say.

Warhol died in 1987, a solid five years before MTV's *The Real World* came into our lives – a show many consider ground zero in the reality show plague that befell the human race. But, his premonition about fame had already come true... well before his death. Game shows had real folks that were milked for any smidge of their whacky personality, *Candid Camera* caught the general public in goofy and embarrassing situations, and the TV news was a prime spot to find every day folks interviewed about what crime they just witnessed and how they felt about things in the world like gas rate hikes and local government decisions -- regardless of how uneducated they were. Even shows like NBC's *Real People*, a show that spotlighted every day folks doing everyday things, and *That's Incredible*, ABC's answer that showcased human nature's more extreme people in a *Ripley's Believe It Or Not!*-style showcase, pre-dated reality TV by a decade or two. These shows featured humans who pushed the limits of their bodies, prompting the producers to place DO NOT TRY THIS AT HOME warnings across the screen.

Surely Andy couldn't know the Kardashians would be on television for 20 years and he probably never foresaw a show where hot, tattooed studs and vixens dated on a Mexican beach through the process of elimination roses. But, he probably had a pretty good idea. He was a visionary after all.

Unfortunately, the warning of "do not try this at home" did not resonate with anyone. Perhaps the warning should have been "do not try this on TV." Because as the years have gone on, more and more every day folks have crept onto our regularly scheduled programming guides. With 500 cable channels to fill and endless streaming services competing for your eyeballs, they've turned to the idea of turning on a camera and pointing it at anyone who happens to pass in front of it. They'll film rich people, poor people, tiny people and morbidly obese people trying to lose weight. They spotlight ghost hunters, Big Foot chasers, wilderness survivalist and alligator wranglers. They have film crews on fishing boats, crews in caves excavating for gold, and crews following crews trying to unlock the mysteries of Unidentified Flying Objects. This represents a fraction of what's on the reality TV plate. The meat of the reality meal is in pairing people into relationships. The dating scene, one of humankinds most discomforting train wrecks, is brought to life in full HD to your living room so you can partake in each soul-crushing crash-and-burn exchange. They'll talk about their terrible lives, their head-scratching fetishes and reveal their outdated personal manifestos that could alert either a priest or the FBI to come running to help. These participants will date on the beach, they'll date by the pool, they'll date in a mansion and they'll come across as completely natural even though they're being hounded by a film crew of 18 people as well as producers feeding them lines of dialogue.

What's painfully clear about all of these people is they're all too real. They're painfully dull, mind-numbingly uneducated and unattractive in a way that is hard to quantify. Beauty is in the eye of the beholder, but the faces plastered onto the screen have an ugliness that is soul deep. Buckets of makeup and poor hairstyle choices are surface level, but when combined with shrill, monstrous personalities accompanied by complete lack of self-awareness, the combination will make you recoil in terror. If you were in a prison cell with these people you'd beg for solitary confinement. Maybe a month in a black box will get you in touch with yourself so you can contemplate your viewing choices.

Warhol and Waters kept company with a bounty of

scallywags – but these people were interesting. They were artists, models, filmmakers and a generally fascinating lot – regardless if they ate their own feces or not. They're not just good company, they made life acceptable by bringing a modicum of joy into it. Even if madness crept in along with the joy. The reality TV nation are the opposite. Dull to the point of being a negative, they're essentially black holes of joy. They suck the life out of the viewing public. Their terrible personalities are magnified and presented as quirks, when in reality (no pun intended) every wart has been intensified to the point that it's become the main feature.

Adding jet fuel to the personal jet fires is the slick packaged nature of it all. We've raised a generation of TV producers who can slap gleaming graphics and cool transitions into any scenario. Someone crunching a giant bowl of green salad one minute, and shopping for scented candles the next, can appear to have the life of royalty if between these two scenes a shot of a bikini-clad woman walking a Chihuahua and a glittering shot of a Rolls Royce slide by our eyes to the thumping beat of toe-tapping synth music. In this fabrication even *I* could come across as slightly interesting. One minute I can be typing away on my computer and as I walk to the kitchen for my ninth cup of coffee, scenes of a Rolls Royce tire crushing coffee beans and dumped into the coffee machine by naked princesses using golden tongs could make my life appear much more fascinating that it actually is.

What makes these shows run is the cliffhanger nature of them. Not just episode-to-episode, but from moment to moment. In one scene, someone is yanking a log out of the mud using their pickup truck that is not powerful enough to do the job. We know this because it's been stated multiple times by the owner that: "the truck's engine wasn't built for this type of thing." Right before we cut to commercial, there's shouting and shaky camera work because it looks like it's all going to come flipping over. Cut to commercial. Upon return, it's stated for the 15th time that the: "truck is not built for this type of job" and we essentially start all over again. When revealed completely, the truck pulls the log without issue, the yelling was for nothing, and somehow the producers managed to milk about 10 minutes of TV from about 20 seconds of footage. Truly riveting stuff.

This type of extremeness is only matched by the extreme nature of a show's theme. Just when we've thought all subject matters have been exhausted, along comes someone who married their mother-in-law, or has fallen in love with the second head growing on the side of their husband's face. No subject is too taboo. Some channels are dedicated completely to reality TV, parading any subject they can muster from their magic cauldron of muck. Back in the 1990s during the heyday of trash talk show TV where Jerry Springer and Jenny Jones marched any idiot with a pulse onto a stage, they'd end each show with a plea to send them their mired, poor and grubbing masses yearning to heave. They'd ask: "Are you having a secret relationship with your gay neighbor's dog? call the number on the screen now." I'm sure the phone rang off the hook because these shows ran for decades -- a new carnival act on screen every single day. Reality TV ladles the same mire into our bowls with subjects so ridiculous, we've become immune to their awfulness. Every new show is an attempt to gain a following and hoping an identical mass of people with similar issues appears to support the cause. Blind marriages and polygamy are only the tip of the iceberg. Yank the slot machine handle to see what combination of crazy flips onto the display and hope the combination pays off with a casting call of clowns that march to the beat of that drum. Blind –> Single Moms –> Who Love Serial Killers. Cha-Ching!

More shocking than the cretins on the TV are the people who are fans of them. An 800-pound woman eating herself to death as she rots on her couch is nothing more than a statistic, but jam her on TV and she can reach a celebrity status most 2nd rate thespians who kill themselves at their craft can only hope to achieve in their lifetime. Eventually they write books and make appearances because God knows the nuances of their miserable lives need finer details than the TV is able to display. We need to know their feelings and motivations and their hopes for the future. These reality show morons are only superseded in stupidity by the people who put them on a pedestal. Their adoring public can only hope to achieve a level of stardom their heroes have garnered – showing us the power of fame and it's unspeakable allure. Most people believe they are worthy of being famous, regardless of talent. They want to be adored and loved by strangers, forsaking everything to achieve this. Even though they are talentless, grotesque and offer nothing but pounds of flesh, they want to be the apple of the adoring public's eye. It's a mystery as to why. The only things they've been able to offer is the ability to take up precious space.

The price of fame is what happens on the backend. The news is more than happy to deliver a hot new item for the day. But what about the follow up? Reality TV can shuffle the people into your living room, but what happens when they're all used up? *The where are they now*? Sure, it's funny to watch a couple bicker with their sextuplets, but what happens when the money runs out and the booze costs and doctor's bills go painfully out of control? Yes, the dinner conversations with the family of 18 was funny, but it costs a small fortune to feed these yapping mouths – education costs be damned.

I admit, I'm a sucker for these shows myself. We all are. I know I need a steady diet of vegetables, but I can't live without the occasional splurge on Cheetos. I have my reality shows – my guilty pleasures. I like to watch a couple's relationship go down in flames on a Hawaiian beach as much as the next person. I like documentaries about heavy subjects like the aftermath of war and government corruption. 60 Minutes is an hour of grim reality that can knock you in the teeth. But I can't feed my soul this stuff all the time. I do want to know what happens to a woman whose facelift went so awry, she needed two ribs and slab off flesh from her ass to reconstruct it. Wouldn't you? Vegetables come on a rack… but Cheetos come in a neon bag that glows with magnetism. But, too much and you're belly aches and you have regret. It's time wasted and brain cells forever damaged. Too many of these reality shows and you can see the flipping numbers of your IQ fall before your very eyes.

But, there's also a vicarious nature to it all. Watching the ship go down from the comfort of your living room. The ability to say, "Ouch that looked painful… That's going to leave a mark." then stand up and ask the people in your home if they want a second helping of ice cream. A pie in the face is funny stuff as long as it doesn't happen to you. But where does it stop? How low can it go? Public hangings? Shootings in the face? In 1974, Christine Chubback put a gun to her head and blew her brains out during a live news broadcast. That footage is mysteriously missing. I know because I've searched high and low for it, and I don't have a streaming service subscription to the dark web, where I'm sure it's readily available. In 1996 after an unfortunate episode of *The Jenny Jones* Show where a guest surprised an unsuspecting person as their gay crush, the incensed and enraged Jonathan Schmitz (no relation to me) shot the person who brought him to the show, Scott Amedure, twice in the chest. This is the dark side of reality gone wrong. Although the episode never aired, I'm sure the *Jenny Jones Show* would have killed to have the footage played on a loop. Imagine the ratings!

What is the future of the reality show; the guillotine? Public deaths are not going to be the rage but what about character assassinations? Has everyone read the fine print on the contract? Each participant can see the total of their Instagram followers rapidly rising; but what about their karma totals? When does the toll get paid for that nasty piece of business? You can be riding high in April and shot down in May – depending on how it's handled. In tough competition… whether it's in pursuit of love or the meat of a bear… the ones who are the *nastiest* win the bearskin rug; or walk the red carpet. The more outrageous, the better. Now more than ever we heap praise on those who can push the envelope the furthest. It's water cooler talk. Mean girl business. The squeaky wheel gets the grease, but the screaming bitch will get the contract. Or, at the very least, show up next season as a continuing contestant. *The Prize of Peril* by Robert Sheckley, Stephen King's *The*

Running Man and *The Hunger Games* by Suzanne Collins all depict dystopian societies in which the public drools for an impending bloodlust fulfilled by tossing the average Joe into a cacophonous meat grinder called reality competition. They're not as far-fetched as it seems. Mainly because we've been watching the ultimate reality competitions for the past 100 years. Professional sports... mainly football. Satiating gladiatorial lust already occurs on Sundays with the chance to see someone lose their head with a properly placed hit. And our colloquial coliseum of power to make someone live or die with a thumb up or down can be satisfied by the click of a social media button. If you want to take it all the way to the top, reality TV is on all the time with our 24 news buzz cycle, the pinnacle being our impending sense of armchair doom in the hands of our incompetent, asinine government officials. It's a sledgehammer to the head that will blow your hair back and drop you into a reality so real, it can trigger a slew of terrible anxieties and addictions.

We escape from this ultimate reality by switching off our brains and tuning into the "reality" of these manufactured TV souls and all their dreadful, questionable and laughable decisions. Our hapless heroes will dive headfirst into a love triangle, consequences be damned. They'll have cantaloupe sized boils lanced for your viewing pleasure or recall in great detail how their lip-enhancement nearly cost them their lives. They'll operate on a horses ass after they've presented every reason why their human patients are one too. These icons live off the land, tally up the cost of our belongings, and let them eat cake, all while their clothes are falling, or have fallen all the way off.

It's must watch TV. You can tune in and out as you like. You can leave and never come back... but if you do, they'll still be there... these really *real* people. Where are they going? As long as there's an audience to watch and a constant stream of humans who desire our undivided attention, they'll be there to do a song-and-dance routine on the great big TV... for 15 minutes or for 15 years. It doesn't matter whether you're laughing at them or with them. They wouldn't know the difference. Or even care.

STEP INTO
MY OFFICE

For years I worked a stone's throw away from Times Square – a tipsy skip to the hub of hubbub. It was an endless stream of activity and international connectivity. For lunch, I frequented a Chinese restaurant run by Mexicans. It was next door to a Mexican place run by Chinese people. True story. Did they ever see the irony of the situation? The backwards nature of it all? Surely they saw each other in the back alley behind the kitchens. Did they swap recipes? Switch staff? Did they date and fall in love with each other? Stick a spare rib in a taco? Fry a burrito in a wok?

What is going on in all the little cubby holes of life? What's cooking inside these stores, buildings, offices and kitchens? Who's in there and what are they doing? Do they know what's on the dark side of the moon? Have they ever licked a battery? Do they have regrets? Has the lady sewing the hem of her one millionth dress ever seen God? Has the short order cook, whose dripping with sweat and sliding a stack of pancakes onto a bed of bacon, ever held a true love to his chest, who in turn, told him they can hear the beating of his heart?

On the journey to self-discovery, one says to be on a journey to find themselves, which can occur on foot. Others are in the process of striping away the layers that have formed over time – like a doorjamb covered in thick coats of paint. Strip away the bad education and the social norms and you may find yourself standing there like a naked wisp... a jangling, buzzing, exposed nerve that could explode from a simple touch. What is there to discover about one's self that is not already there? The mirror is a reflection; but are the eyes seeing everything in truth? The ocular vision is filtered through the brain, but the mind is the biggest liar of all... its many chambers and passages hold secrets and tales that other parts don't want you to know. Perhaps this is the journey we walk. The one that goes deep inside.

You can row a boat to a thousand shores, taste all the spices, and gobble drugs like candy, but to go deep inside yourself may expose the storms of your darkest fears that wash you out to a sea of crazy, getting you lost forever. Where you are going may not be as important as who you are. The most thoughtful monks have wondered why we exist and I'm not sure a proper answer has been given. And what if an answer presents itself? Then what? We stop and call it a day? A life? Shut it down? Crank the power off and fold the tents? Perhaps in our desire to not think about the why, we think about the where. We move along at a good clip because to stop is to fall into despair. It's hard to stop the world and get off. It's moving really fast.

The journey to find yourself doesn't stop until they lower you into the ground… either in one chunk or in dusty pieces. Perhaps the journey is less about who you are and more about your desires. Your tastes, your passions, the fulfillment of your dreams. Maybe you don't know a dream because you've yet to discover everything the buffet has to offer. There's Chinese and Mexican… but have you tried the Indian? What about French, or Burmese? Thai and German? Ethiopian? The list goes on.

In movies, there seems to be a glamorous nature in a struggling individual at the bar – clutching a drink and fighting a silent battle with their existence. Maybe they're mumbling through a scenario, or simply going mad. But what happens when that person is you? Not a struggle with the contents in the glass, but a struggle with who you are… or who you are becoming? The bartender may ask if "everything is alright" because it's their job to run a tight ship – reduce the fights, keep the glassware from shattering, and police a general peace in the place. Any answer you give probably comes across as disingenuous. "I'm fine." Pour me another.

Not far from my Chinese/Mexican connection was a grim Dutch/French/Scandinavian bar that hung a flag I never determined what plot of land they pledged alliance to. The interior was decked out with French posters, vintage Guinness ads with a toucan, little triangular World Cup soccer flags strung across the ceiling (which I remember being either two years after the World Cup had ended, or two years too early to start celebrating the next one), and for good measure, a smattering of dark wooden beer taps emblazoned with names in gold paint that had more consonants and accents than a

Czechoslovakian submarine captain. The menu had rich meats, served with strong cheeses and dolloped with potatoes and gravies and the occasional gummy fruit and salty nut – the kind of meal that sticks to your ribs, can be eaten on a tree stump, and is easily sharable with your friendly neighborhood forest faun.

I started hitting the place around lunch when my job started falling apart. Not the actual job itself, but the job environment. In fact, I felt a strong sense of job security, which is probably why I started drinking at lunch. Some people drink at lunch when shit is slipping away, but I was doing OK and that gave me the confidence to knock a few back. My boss was slowly, but surely losing the group. She was a half-wit who could barely string five words together to form a sentence, and when she did, she used words incorrectly. It's actually a great fear of mine to use words incorrectly in a sentence, so I tend to keep my mouth shut. My boss felt completely free to use words incorrectly – a trait of the stupid. They don't get embarrassed because they're too uneducated to know otherwise. And when you're the boss, no one corrects you.

Even though the bar was literally around the corner – mere steps from the front door of my office building, I knew no one would find me there. It wasn't a place you sought out. The place was dark, unassuming. If you didn't look around, you'd pass right by it like the 10 million other places in New York City. It was half a block from Times Square, but no tourist would go there. It didn't have that kind of magnetism. In fact, it may have had a negative charge – bouncing people away. It was a place for the lost and broken. There'd be some people at the back tables, scraping mashed potatoes or flattened meat into their face, but they seemed more like regulars – or perhaps even the owners. Pale-skinned Scandinavians with stark black hair, the occasional tussled blond with round reading glasses, or the lump of old-country frump... a human potato... pre mashed.

There were no Mexicans or Chinese in there. It was usually just me, the occasional stowaway, and the bartender who not only never spoke, but never even said hello. You'd order a drink and in seconds it was there in front of you, then the bartender slid back to the edge of the bar and flipped open a magazine. If you wanted a refill you'd need to ask because they certainly weren't patrolling the bar for empty glasses. It was the perfect place to go and fuck the hell off. To be alone. It was more than alone. It was a black hole. Just another cubby in a series of endless cubbies filled with creatures who were trying to figure out who they were, what the hell they were doing, and where the hell they were going. Or trying to escape those questions.

It was a place I asked those questions, but I never got the answers. No one ever does. Not about life or my job. At my job, me and about five other people were doing the job of 25. I couldn't figure out who was working. There seemed to be an inordinate amount of people doing nothing. An unruly cluster of people un-tethered and improperly managed by the corporate higher-ups. Of course, a lot of people think their workmates are lazy incompetents. Mostly they're correct. It's man's inherent nature to do as little as possible and hope for the best results.

I was contemplating another job offer with more pay, a longer title and I suppose more prestige – whatever that meant. If you work hard and long enough, they stick titles onto your job description until it's longer than your actual name. If you climb the ladder high enough and murder a good selection of people along the way, the job title becomes an acronym.

I saw my current work nest coming apart, but I actually liked it, so I didn't want to leave. But, I figured I should get while the gettin' was good. So I did.

•••

I had a year under my belt at the new gig and was more lost than the last gig. It was a longbow shot from the United Nations building – more international than the Times Square area, but somehow more gentrified. It was a wash of steakhouses and German food. I couldn't locate a decent bar anywhere. There was a German beer hall, but it was louder than a football game and not conducive to sitting quietly and contemplating the confusing and ridiculous world we die in.

There was a German fusion restaurant right down the street on the corner. That's a term you don't hear very often. The German's aren't known for their wild diversity. In fact, they're known for the stubborn inflexibility. It's why they make great cars and guns, but don't exactly lead the world in culinary delights. This joint had exotic schnitzels with noodles and potato pancakes, but they served it all in square boxes printed with a fancy name, so that emboldened them to charge twice as much for it. But, their biggest issue was they didn't serve beer, and any German worth his brine will tell you to goose-step it right on out of there.

My only choice was to hit an Irish pub around the corner. Any further and I'd need to leave the hood. It was right on 3rd avenue. Bend your neck at the correct angle... or, pass out on the bartop, and you could see the Chrysler Building. The place was the opposite of what was needed. It was downright chipper, full of lunchers who wanted to talk. The atmosphere was light and bright. Practically glowing. Most Irish pubs have their fair share of red-nosed drunks, clustered into a dark atmosphere that grows mushrooms and moss. This place could grow pineapples it was so damn bright.

My inner thoughts didn't fester very well there. I needed to know who I was and where I was going... again. I'd left a job and arrived at this job, but was lost again.

When people say they need to find themselves, they think it's a long journey... a walk around the world, a religious enlightenment or a lightning bolt realization. But the finding of yourself isn't an outside key that will unlock a door to your soul. The key is already there... inside you. In life, we obtain all the information we can absorb until we hit an apex – a tipping point where we need to stop and reassess what we've taken in. Because we lack better terminology we call it finding ourselves, when in reality, it's digging. Imagine being pasted over with papers. Thousands of papers. It's your life – photos, quotes, people you've loved and those that have hurt you... embarrassing situations, failures and soaring success. It's your job at this point, whether your 30 or 40 or 55 years of age, to filter through it and decide what works for you and what can be discarded. A purge. Only when you begin to remove the layers of bad education, useless philosophies and the ideals that others have displaced upon you, can you begin to find yourself. The finding of yourself is not out there – it's inside. You've been buried under piles of conditions and you need to remove them. You've always been there, you just haven't properly filtered through the mess.

If we're to say that we're finding ourselves, then perhaps it's true. We're finding ourselves under the piles of things that have been stacked on top of us for decades. Like buried treasure. If *that* is finding ourselves, then perhaps the adage is true. But the journey begins not on a path, but on an inward trajectory. The organization of thoughts, beliefs that are yours through experience, and the ability to not care what others think… philosophies built through time. But, other things get in the way. Outside influences that are hard to reject.

Every piece of information that enters you changes you in some way. You can run at top speed but when the hands of life push you, your course takes a new trajectory. Sometimes those trajectories have stops and I've found myself at many waiting stations. Sometimes you don't figure this out till you've traveled all over the place and settled down.

My new boss was competent. More than competent, she was very good… could form sentences and use words correctly in a statement. She had hands the size of oven mitts… so meaty, she could work an oil rig. She could easily cup one hand around my entire skull like a baseball. When I first noticed them, she was writing some directions on a piece of paper and the pen practically disappeared into the fist like a toothpick. I couldn't believe the sheer size of them. I never mentioned anything because I'm sure she knew very well she had man-hands. But, who was I too judge? I have bony hands cabled with thick, blue veins – the kind you might find wrapped around a stick while it's stirring a witch's cauldron.

Even though I was getting paid more, I downgraded from a group of 5 people among 25 people doing the work of 25 people, to an actual group of 5 people doing the work of 25 people. We were overworked and understaffed. I was constantly being introduced to people who "worked" with us… only I never worked with them, or saw them again. I don't know if they were freelance, or if they were on the way in, or out, or if it was all just a series of rotating craziness, but I never felt secure in the job and I realized quickly in my desire to move forward, I moved backwards.

There was no place to hide anymore. At the old place, we had our own floor and I had my own office. Now I was mixed with different departments in cubicles with no walls. I was naked for all to see. Any webpage I scrolled, regardless of content, was displayed like a Times Square billboard. I had just left Times Square. We had a snitch bitch on the floor in the accounting department who felt entitled to wander about and note every infraction – disregarding the fact she wasn't doing her own damn job. Every Facebook status check, every phone call or text sent and received, was noted and registered like the Gestapo. Before long, my infractions had risen to the point of needing a face-to-face with the boss. I was being written up – like some rotten child.

When my infractions spilled into the street, that's when it all fell apart. I was spied in a bar… the glittering, bright-as-headlights Irish bar I despised. The bitch saw me there knocking back a beer, solidifying my stance on the necessity of hidden bars with limited windows and lighting a smidge above blackout drunk.

I was gone soon after. Not from drinking in bars, but from the utter lack of structure in the place. The place wasn't being run so much as being run into the ground. There's a phrase for a business that is running while also rebuilding: *building the airplane while it's in the air*. That situation was more like duct-taping a homemade go-cart as it was diving off a cliff – while on fire.

•••

Eventually I got on a runaway train that stopped at City Hall. The number 6 train on the green line. Might as well have dropped me off in the middle of Mars. It felt that alien.

My new office was a strong spit from the City Hall building in lower Manhattan. Lean your greasy forehead against the floor-to-ceiling window in my boss's office and you could see it. My office was across from a dark brick building with complicated architecture that no one ever saw but me. It was certainly never seen from the street and I wasn't quite sure why it was built. Maybe at one time it was the apple of the neighborhoods' eye, but now it was another dark tomb, stacked against other tombs that shaded the streets below into a cold, grey ant farm.

The area consisted mostly of high-end shoppers, government groups and Wall Street douchebags – a most sorted collection of two-faced ass-fucks if there ever was one. Even though the area was vintage, old-school Manhattan with thin sidewalks, ancient buildings and tight crowded roads, the place oozed as much charm as having a diesel tailpipe rammed down your throat till the exhaust puffed out your ears like the black cloud of a crematorium chimney.

Every swinging dick you saw was on a phone making a deal, and those who weren't, pretended to be on the phone making a deal because that's what self-important sociopaths do. It was a stunning array of back-stabbers and vampires who turn the screws of everyone they see until they're bled completely dry – whether it's a bank account or actual blood.

This was the financial heartbeat of the planet where those CEOs, COOs, and other acronymed dipshits and entitled leaders of companies need to make yearly cuts to feed the ever-hungry beast that is their own greed. They have no qualms about slashing the jobs of good, hard-working people with children and mountains of hospital bills so they can inflate their bonuses into the six-figure range. These animals would happily push an old lady down a flight of stairs, then walk across her back to avoid getting blood on their $1,900 handmade Italian leather shoes that she's carelessly coughing up from her broken esophagus. By the time anyone figures it all out, the boss has used his fat bonus to re-trim the brass on his 85-foot yacht. And be thankful you didn't stop THAT necessity from happening by "mucking up the process" because he would hire some recent prison-released malcontent to have your family hacked to pieces with a cleaver if you stood in his way.

This toxic attitude explodes from the aura of every person like dynamite. To bump into them is to be in a real-world pinball machine. A clanging, jangling, sonorous showdown. The only way to avoid them is to walk in the streets with the cars, or dip into a quiet bar – the preferable choice. Unfortunately no real oasis exists down there. Even the dive bars are loaded with the auras of dynamite. No matter how quiet the dive is, a few suited, zooted, moneyed zippidy-do-das pile in to drink their problems away and soon the place is buzzing like the trading floors.

There's no rest for the weary in those noisy halls. There's no place to reach any kind of Zen; or a false interpretation of Zen; or to contemplate trying to settle into a state to begin on the road to Zen. The eyes of the people in the shops and little cubby holes looked just as lost as me. Their eyes a million miles away. Their eyes locked onto the next step in life. Their bed, their TV, the arms of their spouse or at the bottom of a bottle. They certainly didn't want to be there – steaming our lunch, cooking our laundry, or gluing something together... the never-ending working hands of time, perpetually operating something, working towards a paycheck that was never enough and gave little or no satisfaction.

There was a Vietnamese sandwich shop I frequented. Had the best chicken sandwich I ever ate. Place was smaller than my closet. Had five tables that were always full. They played blockbuster movies at deafening levels on the tiny TV that sat on a refrigerator. The girls were cute, piling sandwiches like 3D puzzles. I'd take my lunch outside but there was no place to sit. Every square inch rose to the sky in the form of a building and any horizontal space had foot or street traffic. So, I gave up and ate at my desk.

The only places to find liquid refuge was in a trendy bar or tavern and they were all overpriced watering holes where the auras of dynamite would yap endlessly about their portfolios, golf games and who they were currently fucking over. They were making deals over cocktails, barking at each other like rabid dogs, and generally not listening to what the other person was saying because what THEY were saying was far more important. I couldn't drink there. Not only was it loud, but, there was never any open spots. Guys who couldn't make deals over lunch, made deals at the bar. By the time they realized they were completely hammered, they skipped the table reservation and fed themselves where they sat.

So to find solace, I did the most rational thing I could do. I started smoking a pipe. Yes, a pipe. Not a crack pipe – although it would have been preferable – but a good old-fashioned wooden tobacco pipe. The kind you saw in the 1950s pecked into dad's mouth after he got home from work, sat in his lay-z-boy chair, unwrapped the newspaper and drained five whiskeys. It was a rich, cherry wood pipe, carved in a prince style. Basically a normal pipe that curved down a bit, but with the bowl returning up till it was horizontal. Modest and sleek.

I bought the pipe from a haberdashery a few paces away from my apartment. It was an old-school place that was dying off like many other old-school New York spots. They sold pipes, lighters, cigars, pocket knives, wallets, tweed hats, pocket watches, and a slew of other items you might find dangling off some fancy gentleman riding around on his Penny-farthing bicycle. When I saw the cigar and pipe shop a few blocks away from my office while searching for safe haven, I resurrected the pipe and made the humidor my new home.

When I entered, the smoke hung chest-level like post-cannon fire. Every person in the place had some variation of broiling stick corked in their mouth. A young employee, skinny and frantic like me, smoked a full bent pipe while working the register – something Sherlock Holmes may have gravitated towards. In a few short years, he'd be hacking like a cancer patient, but he seemed healthy and upright at that moment. People came in and out like Grand Central Station during the rush. They purchased stogies, brown cigarettes and everything that caught fire. The place had a wall of heavy, lidded glass jars – the kind you find in a mad scientist's lab with human heads swimming inside. All of them filled with pipe weed, labeled and scratched in handwriting with names like Chesapeake and Arrow Creek. Things that evoked languid days blowing smoke rings on Bilbo's Shire.

I got an ounce of something smooth and retired to the humidor – a glass box with lush carpet and recliner seats. It was like my father's country club locker room, the hangout where they played cards and talked about the hole placement on 15. It was quiet in there, all the guys sitting back, honking on ridiculous logs of rolled tobacco. I took a seat at a game table in a leather padded wooden chair. I stuffed my pipe, but realized I didn't have a lighter, so I sparked it with matches that someone left in the angular glass amber ashtray. There was only three matches remaining in the worked-over book, so I lit my pipe carefully. This wasn't the environment to ask for a light. These men were in deep thought; escaping their miserable lives and tabulating their crushing loses. The room was cool and the air-filter worked overtime. A giant muted TV ran the Wall Street numbers and the talking heads nodded at each other's sage advice. The TV glowed cartoon hues into my eyes, but my mind wandered inside myself. No one in the room spoke. Not even coughed, an occurrence you'll find unusual in a room packed with carcinogenic air.

I let the smoke roll in my mouth and occasionally let a deep inhale buzz me into an alternate universe. I was at that place again. The crossroads of life. I was working, but the writing was on the wall already. This job wouldn't stick. My boss was fine. I never saw him. I assumed his sentence structure was adequate and his vocabulary acceptable. My workmates were competent. No one was throwing anyone under the bus; literally or metaphorically. But the future was set. It didn't take a prognosticator to see that the place wasn't for me. Didn't take a drunk or a smoke-filled asshole to figure it out either. I was like a Spanish swordsman riding in a tribe of cut-throat Vikings. Or maybe I was the Viking and they were the Spanish swordsmen. Doesn't matter. I didn't fit. They can sense that type of thing, like dogs who can smell drugs or the strange woman I see on the news who can smell Parkinson's Disease or Alzheimer's. They can sense you don't fit shortly after you've walked in the door. Once the dust has settled from the interview process where everyone was on their best behavior and not acting like a neurotic dipshit with a loaded gun in their hand, that's when the true colors start to show. I didn't want to be there and they didn't want me.

But, where did I fit? Who was I... you get the point.

Months later, there I was, at the end, sitting in what can only be described as the den in the first order of hell. I had the smoke drenched clothing to prove it – pumping away at the pipe. Glassy-eyed and confused. The quiet eye of the storm. Surrounded by a swirling mass of madness in the bowels of lower Manhattan – an island that was no longer dirt, but a twisted amalgamation of cables, wires, pipes and tubes, all baked into a cement cake that acted as a foundation to support the towering man-made stalagmites, filled with cubby holes for all the people and their tragic and beautiful stories.

On the search for new discovery, I peeled off so many layers that I stood as bare as stripped wood against the elements. Exposed and without anything else to lie about. I couldn't stay in these jobs because there was an obvious sense of needing to be somewhere else. Somewhere that fed my soul or could be a lightning rod to my talent, vision or general frustration. Most could see I was checked out long before I could. On the journey to self-discovery, I found myself lost on an island with no resources, other than the occasional cold beer and warm pipe.

The faking of enthusiasm can only last so long, and at some point, you'll be required to pledge your loyalty, or at the very least, your dedication to the cause. If you're not all in, committed, drinking the Kool-Aid and surrendering to the vision, you might as well be the madman banging on the pulpit for the new world order. It's painfully obvious you're that much of a black sheep. It appears as subtlety, but shine the spotlight on the perpetrator and they freeze like ice, guilty on all accounts of being all-out, undedicated, uncommitted, skating by, doing the bare minimum and only doing just enough to add fuel to the hungry furnace that burns everything in its brutal, insatiable mouth... consuming time, money, bills and your dreams. A vacuum that has no prejudice in the great scheme of things. A unabashed judge of all that exists, laying waste to every color and creed and grinding everyone into dust to place them harshly, without favor into the starving dirt to become the fertilizer of tomorrow's growing misery.

When you're caught in the cog of the machine, it's your desire to get out as quickly as possible, hoping another machine will run smoother – but they rarely do. It's all part of the same machine. The gears are connected even though they seem like they're far apart. Maybe you dream of dropping off the machine, like a loose nut that wasn't adhered correctly on a bicycle assembled on Christmas Eve. One of the five screws that didn't seem to matter because the bike functioned completely normal. But loose nuts can roll away forever, never to find a groove that fastens it to something solid. They end up in the junk drawers of life and never find a home until they're tossed away, forgotten like the garbage the trash man hauled away last week.

•••

I finally found my drinking spot, right around the corner from my apartment. I liked it, although it didn't have any sense of Zen calmness. They made the best chicken wings in town, so it was constantly crowded. I didn't have a job to pay for them, so I just drank. I could sit at the bar and watch the 5 screaming TVs or sit at the railing by the window and watch the world go by. Depending on my mood, I rotated. The bar spot would eventually get a person in my ear yapping about their troubles. The window was quiet and nobody bothered me there. The world went by in a blur at the window. The traffic, the people, the suburban girls desperately looking for a husband – their faces wide in scan mode, trying to lock eyes with a man so he could fall in love with them and drag them out to the suburbs so they could produce children and never have to think about city life again.

The bar wasn't near any major tourist attractions, famous architectural structures, or places that catered to the fragments of human existence. These patrons were exactly what I needed – neighborhood types. Quiet, sometimes interesting, occasionally loud. On Sunday the place exploded with football. I would go and catch a quarter or two until I needed real quiet, then I'd venture uptown to a dark bar on York. Never knew how it stayed in business. No one was ever there. Big and cavernous with olive green walls, heavy wooden tables and chairs strewn about. It had a long bar that could easily fit 25. Huge back mirror. Was probably a restaurant at one time, but they didn't serve food… or cheer. I liked a good dive, but this was more like a waiting room. Joyless. But definitely quiet. Perhaps a waiting room to the next level, which may have been death.

I'd just left a box and was searching for another box. A box that paid me a salary. And perhaps that was my problem. I didn't fit inside certain boxes – containers that could contain. They were prisons. Prisons of the mind for sure. Prisons to the soul, no doubt. I was willing to give up certain freedoms if I got something else in return… spiritual enlightenment… satisfaction in the form of artistic release… maybe the occasional orgasm that carried me along for a while. I didn't consider myself some untamed soul. A self-proclaimed poet of the streets who needed an audience to follow them on some cosmic awakening. I was willing to accept the little satisfactions the world sometimes offers. Good coffee on a rainy day. A face full of sunshine at the beach. The answer to life's questions delivered by angels in the form of a whisper spoken gently into my ear.

So where does the spirit lie? Can it get satisfaction from the little things in life? Or is it a constant game of grasping at straws that life hands out in a cruel game of "what are you going to get?" At some point you may need to surrender. Wave the white flag. You can enter the cage, cell, jail, office or container of your choice, but it may not be ideal. Unfortunately, when you lock yourself inside to be part of the system, the mind wanders further and further away. The closer the hands are chained to the desk, the more wayward the mind gets. The hands are not only locked, they solidify... become one with whatever is holding them. Then the mind drifts to the sky. Eventually the wood of the desk creeps up the arms and past the elbows. Then the mind drifts into space. Soon the whole body is one solid block of composite wood and plastic fibers. And the mind... it's gone to an alternate universe. A place with alien creatures. Translucent skin and a thousand eyes. They slide and absorb one another like amoebas. They have no answers because there's no questions. They're having the beautiful life you want. They have no money system. No government. No rules. No stress.

But one of them ultimately breaks away – becomes unabsorbed and gets hold of a device. A device that can see millions of light years away and they put one of their thousand eyes into the device... a telescope of some sort, and they focus on us and see the people in their cubby holes. Living their crazy lives, moving around in a frenzied state. And the alien wonders who they are. What they are doing? Do they like the smell of gasoline? Do they enjoy the feeling of getting into bed after taking their socks off? Have they ever felt the impending doom of their mortality creep up on them while in the middle of a conversation about donuts?

Then the telescope focuses on me.

They zoom in.

"Who is that?" they ask.

"Where is he going?"

www.ingramcontent.com/pod-product-compliance
Lightning Source LLC
Chambersburg PA
CBHW060909120626
46553CB00001B/264